Megan
John

FASHION FUTURES

FOR FRAN

FASH ION FUTU RES

BRADLEY QUINN

MERRELL
LONDON · NEW YORK

INTRODUCTION

As designers and other practitioners transform the traditions of the past into fresh inspiration for the present, they signpost bold new directions for the fashions of the future

Robotic skins, microelectronic circuits, conductive threads and supple sensors may sound like the hallmarks of computer science, but in the hands of designers and technologists they are the raw materials for some of the most avant-garde garments produced today. When these materials are combined with high-tech textiles, they can be crafted into the fabric keyboards and wearable computer systems that are shaping the fashions of the future. Not only are such interactive technologies changing the ways in which garments are designed and worn, but also they are radically reforming the way fashion is manufactured and sold.

Future fashions will reflect the participatory, networked societies in which we live today, with online social networks, blogs and GPS-enabled forums making it possible to share experiences online and manage real-life meetings from a virtual platform. Fashion has yet to play a significant role in this cultural shift: although interactive technology and communications devices have been present in mobile devices and built structures for some time, few fashion brands have integrated into their products the communications technology and microelectronic systems that can make clothing interactive.

History is marked by the styles of dress developed throughout time. Some of them were born of technology, but most were distinct from it. Despite the dramatic developments now taking place in other design disciplines, few far-reaching innovations have yet taken hold in the fashion industry. Most fashion items continue to be cut out in pieces of cloth that are stitched together,

just as they were at the onset of the Industrial Revolution in the eighteenth century, and fashion students still follow the time-honoured practice of draping fabric against the body before cutting out the pattern in toile (plain cotton cloth) so that the design can be tested. Most of the designers featured in this book have broken with such traditions in order to align fashion practice with new techniques developed in the fields of industrial design or engineering. Many have teamed up with technologists to integrate electronic parts into the garments they design, while others are creating a new synergy between garment and wearer on many different levels.

Wearable technology will enable the garments of the future to be more in tune with their environment, and will allow the senses to play a greater role in everyday experience than they do today. Humans perceive the world through sensory input, and future garments will have the ability to heighten our perception of our bodies and the environments in which we live. They will enable us to identify radio frequencies (for wireless communication) and detect magnetic fields (which can also be used for communications, and to demarcate boundaries); they will sense the presence of invisible pollutants and guide us directly to the objects we seek. Advanced materials will make the fabrication of future clothing as sustainable as the garments will be durable, comfortable and beautiful. Many garments will be designed by their wearers, and most will be manufactured by consumers themselves, who will produce them from files downloaded from designers' websites.

This book charts these developments and many others, outlining some of the key movements that are shaping the industry's future. The fusion

In her Kinetic Landscapes collection for Spring/Summer 2012, Pauline van Dongen designed sleek clothing characterized by fluid contours, geometric cuts and abstract shapes. These give the garments a timeless feel, leading to the conclusion that strong lines are likely to continue to underpin good design.

Malaysian designer Bernard Chandran creates clothing with a vision of launching the fashions of the future. Chandran sets out to design garments that stand out and heighten the wearer's sense of style. Shown here is a piece from his Autumn/Winter 2011–12 collection.

of wearable technology and advanced materials, and the integration of computer parts into fashion items, promise to make clothing that will be perpetually online and maintenance-free. Fashion's emerging alignment with health care will create clothing that diagnoses physical problems and medicates wearers through the skin, delivering vitamins and nutrients that make them feel refreshed. High-performance, protective clothing will heighten wearers' sense of individual security and equip them with the means to safeguard their valuables and their personal data. As future clothing creates intimate refuges from the stresses of everyday life, our garments will also provide solutions for many of the dilemmas we face today.

This book is written at a pivotal moment in the evolution of fashion, in which garments are becoming sensory enough to gauge the wearer's needs and respond accordingly. The book begins by charting some of the ways in which fashion and technology are coming closer together, and by looking ahead to a time when the two will be conceived as one single, wearable unit. Chapter two, 'Power and Performance', highlights the increasing significance of protective clothing, outlining the role that such sciences as biomimicry will play in

performance sportswear, combat uniforms and future street styles. Chapter three, 'Maverick Materials', explores some of the materials that are creating new possibilities for fashion today, and features some of the groundbreaking garments that find applications for them.

Chapter four, 'Future Fabrication', explores how virtual designs, co-creative platforms and novel production methods are forging new directions for fashion manufacturing. Chapter five, 'Radical Retail', outlines some of the innovations taking place in fashion retail today: digital dressing rooms, pop-up boutiques and online forums may replace high-street shops in years to come. The final chapter, 'Future Horizons', examines the role that trends will play in the future. The chapter also identifies twenty influential directions for future fashion, showing their relevance to the wardrobes of tomorrow.

Each chapter concludes with interviews with leading designers and researchers, who share their views of fashion's future in their own words. As they, and other practitioners, transform the traditions of the past into fresh inspiration for the present, they signpost bold new directions for the fashions of the future.

EXTRE STYLE

TAILORING AND TECHNOLOGY
FASHIONING THE MACHINE
WEARABLE INTELLIGENCE
THE EXPERIENCE OF FASHION
FASHION IN THE FIFTH DIMENSION
SENSORY SURFACES
SHIFTING SILHOUETTES

Interviews with
IRIS VAN HERPEN
STUDIO XO

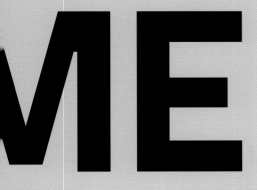

ME

Together, fashion and technology are finding new uses for traditional materials and techniques, while also inspiring new types of tailoring and high-tech fashion fabrics

Technology and fashion are a perfect match. The fast-paced progress of technology complements fashion's ever-evolving aesthetic, and each gives the other a wider frame of reference and more scope to explore new horizons: when associated with garments, which are by nature portable, wireless technology becomes even more mobile, and as technologized fashions wirelessly connect garments to remote systems, they extend both their own functionality and technology's reach. Together, the two are finding new uses for traditional materials and techniques, while also inspiring new types of tailoring and high-tech fashion fabrics.

The way in which we experience fashion is changing, and it promises to be dramatically different in the future. A new generation of designers is envisioning the forms, shapes and materials of tomorrow, transforming garments from passive receivers into active technological tools. Tailoring techniques are aligning with communications technology, exploring the extent to which surface embellishments and decorative detail can provide new ways of transmitting data. Radical reinterpretations of garment design are giving rise to revolutionary new silhouettes, with surfaces that have new functions, and are providing greater potential for creative expression. As shape-shifting technologies integrated into garments radically reinvent the outlines of the body, they also change the way the wearers interact with the spaces surrounding them.

A new dialogue between body and dress is unfolding right now, driven by fashion's potential to function as technological device. The texts in this chapter chart many of the innovations young designers are pioneering today, revealing that the fashions of the future may be analogous to wearable machines. Fashion is starting to move beyond traditional craft techniques and to embrace the wireless future, making it one of the present day's most visionary expressions of technology.

As demonstrated by this outfit from her Escapism collection (Autumn/Winter 2011–12), Iris van Herpen's clothes are characterized by strong shapes and extraordinary silhouettes. The Dutch designer's work is inspired by ideas about the human body's future evolution, and fabricated using advanced materials and pioneering new processes. Van Herpen's interview appears on page 50.

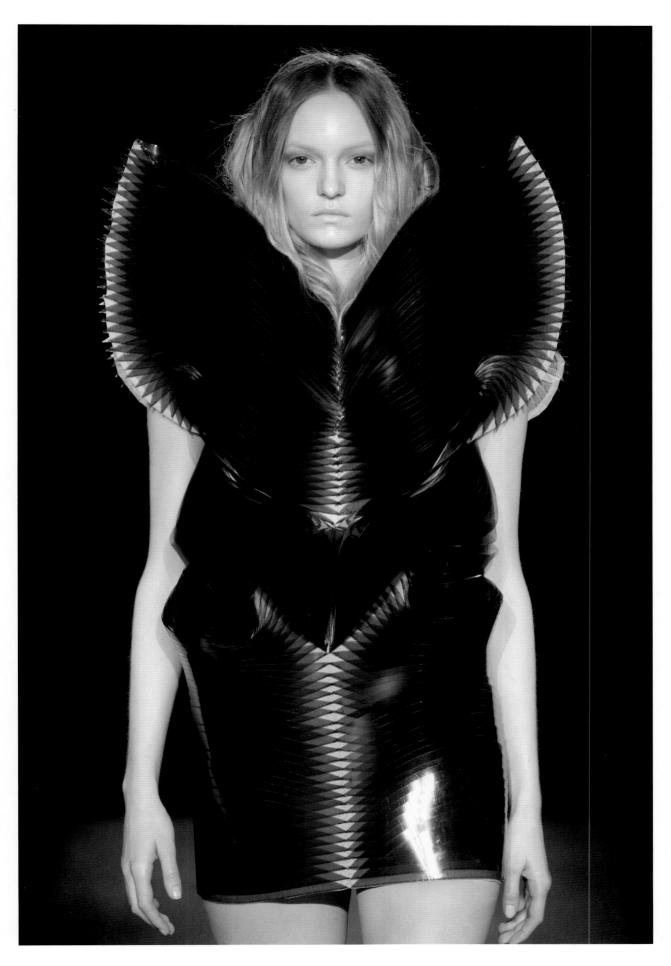

TAILORING AND TECHNOLOGY

Technology has always been the essence of fashion. Although the word 'tailoring' dates back to the thirteenth century, the craft as we know it today did not appear until the 1500s, when the wide skirts, puffed sleeves and voluminous garments in vogue at the time required complex constructions to enable them to hold their shape. Such devices as the corset and the crinoline were crafted from lightweight, flexible materials that could mould the body into dramatic silhouettes. The craftsworkers who created them incorporated basic knowledge of hydraulics and cantilevering into the designs, making tailoring as much a field for technological innovation as an arena for style.

Technological advances continue to underpin tailoring, taking garment design and manufacturing methodologies dramatically forward. Savile Row and science fiction are coming closer on many levels, to the extent that clothing can now be computerized, and computers can be made as garments and actually worn. Electronic fibres capable of conducting electrical impulses can transmit data between microelectronic components and connectors that have been seamlessly integrated into cloth. They enable garments to function as computing devices that relay information via tiny conductors, circuits, silicon chips and sensors, and exchange data with remote systems via transmitters and woven antennae.

Today good tailoring is often regarded as an expensive 'extra', a luxury that represents superior fit, high-quality treatment of cloth and hand craftsmanship. As new automated processes and computerized techniques start to replace human skills, future notions of what tailoring can achieve will be radically different from current ones. Such innovations as laser-cut fabric technology, body scanning and nanotechnology (technology on an atomic or molecular scale) are being combined with temperature-sensitive textiles, no-wash fabrics and phase-change materials (which store and release heat; see page 119), using state-of-the-art technology to improve performance as well as fit. Embellishments, such as lace, can be laser-cut from the garment's base fabric rather than sewn on as trim, for a more efficient use of material.

INTELLIGENT CLOTHING

The first wearable computer prototypes emerged during the early 1990s. The devices were attached to jackets, waistcoats and vests rather than integrated into the garment's fabric, and their cables and connectors were anchored in place by fasteners and stitching, or trailed along seams, collars and cuffs. Such gadgets as the MP3 player were among the first to be partially embedded in textiles, with their wiring and hardware encased between layers of fabric. Wearing these garments with embedded interfaces proved to be awkward and uncomfortable, sparking the demand for a new generation of electronic devices that could be fully integrated into clothing.

Parallel to the development of these wearable gadgets, scientists were researching portable diagnostic health-care systems, while military experts were developing technologically enhanced combat gear. One of the first, and most groundbreaking, examples of diagnostic technology was the Smart Shirt, developed from 1996 by Sundaresan Jayaraman, a professor at the Georgia Institute of Technology, and funded by DARPA (the Defense Advanced Research Projects Agency), the primary research and development arm of the United States Department of Defense. The garment

When it comes to tailoring the female form, British designer Gareth Pugh is considered to be a master of cuts and styles. Pugh works with the symmetry of the body to craft flattering folds and sleek, body-hugging panels. His asymmetrical designs (shown here are pieces from Pugh's Spring/Summer 2011 collection) create new expressions of volume and form.

PAGES 16–17
Californian Rick Owens's
collection for Spring/Summer
2011 presented a strikingly
contemporary vision of
traditional draping. Owens
wrapped fabric around the
body in sleek panels and
streamlined folds that played
with the body's symmetry.

OPPOSITE
Iris van Herpen's Escapism
collection (Autumn/Winter
2011–12) was a tour de force
of tailoring and technology.
Traditional cutting and draping
techniques were superseded
by digital design tools, while
3D printing processes replaced
conventional stitching and
seaming. The collection
underscored the relevance
of advanced digital design
and 3D printing techniques
to couture fashion.

was designed to monitor the movements of the wearer and calibrate heart rate, respiration and body temperature, and to relay the data to a remote system for analysis. Jayaraman interwove lightweight wiring and sensors with natural fibres to create a supple fabric substrate that he fashioned into a sportswear-style shirt.

Although the diagnostic garments pioneered by Jayaraman and other researchers are far removed from the clothing made by the fashion industry, the technological know-how underpinning them was eventually applied to a new style of technologized clothing. Known initially as 'technofashion', 'techwear' or 'intelligent clothing', and referred to today as 'fashionable technology' or 'wearables', the garments are developed according to technological principles yet created in styles that follow fashion trends. Teams formed by technologists and fashion designers are pioneering clothing with the drape, flexibility and resilience of most fashion garments, and that is engineered to be durable, lightweight and flame-resistant. Such collaboration combines the traditionally female practices of garment-making with the previously male-dominated worlds of technology and materials science. The synergy between them is opening up new possibilities for each.

As practitioners from the fields of fashion design and technology come together, they are developing ways in which we can interface with our computers more comfortably. Computers and laptops

have become more user-friendly in recent years, but they still currently restrict the user to a seated or standing posture, and limit interaction to the fingertips. Fashion designers have skills that can make computers more user-friendly still: by sharing their knowledge of body proportions and postures, as well as their insight into the roles of tactility and touch, they can suggest ways in which the entire body can be involved in computer interaction.

With computers fully integrated into garments, in the future clothing may be just another means of storing data. Garments could contain a wide array of sensors and micromachines, as well as such devices as accelerometers, gyroscopes and detectors that pinpoint their location. Concerns about the health risks associated with wearing batteries and transformers in close proximity to the body are motivating researchers to make them more streamlined so that they can be placed on the garment's surface. Positioning them on the outer layer makes it easier for them to harness solar energy and distribute it efficiently throughout the garment.

As garments are redefined as mobile networked environments, they transform the intimate sphere of the human into a means of accessing networks of ideas situated across time and space. Although today garments are conceived as individual structures, the technological interfaces that will characterize them in the future will make them part of global systems.

FASHIONING THE MACHINE

New types of clothing are creating new patterns of behaviour. Garments are beginning to absorb communications technology, and IT systems are becoming embedded in the clothing we wear. Technologists use state-of-the-art materials to make computer parts lightweight and portable, while fashion designers apply tailoring principles to integrate them into clothing. Interactive media is changing the way we live and relate to one another, but soon it will also transform the way we use our clothing.

The new generation of high-tech fashion fabrics will challenge conventions of clothing construction. Sustainable textiles inspired by biomimicry (biomechanical processes; see pages 66–73) will thicken in autumn and slim down in spring, making linings and layers unnecessary. Garments made by traditional means are likely to morph and reconfigure in response to electronic signals that travel along their conductive fibres, creating areas of strain as they do so.

Some innovations are created with the aim of prolonging the garments' lifespan. Forever-clean fabrics and 'sweatproof' shirts will transform clothing from wash-and-wear into self-clean or no-wash. As a result, seams will stop twisting out of shape and detailing will no longer fray or disintegrate, making clothes look fresher for longer and giving them an extended life. This is likely to mean that well-tailored garments may prevail, while throwaway chic may go out of style forever.

The unspoken assumption of all fashion design is that it results in a 'finished' garment. Future fashions, such as the 'growable' garments of the Biocouture initiative (page 141), will continually question this principle, asking if a garment can ever be considered wholly complete:

LEFT AND BELOW
In collaboration with American company Oriole Mill, Despina Papadopoulos of Studio 5050 (see page 36) developed methods of incorporating conductive threads in a jacquard loom. The fashion textiles that result can transmit electronic signals, combining advanced fibre technology with natural materials and hand craftsmanship.

OPPOSITE
Maggie Orth, director of Seattle-based technology research laboratory International Fashion Machines, creates technologized textiles for fashion, interior design and artworks. Many of her pieces change patterns and colourways; this one, created as part of her 100 Electronic Art Years series, contains fifty handmade textile pixels.

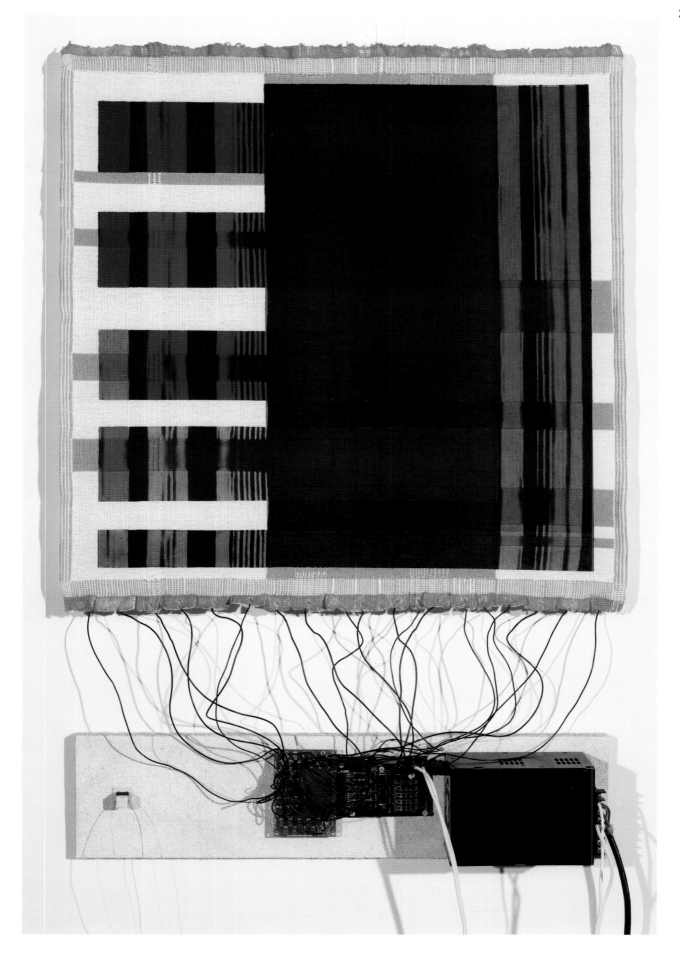

PAGES 22–23
As designers embed light-emitting diodes, fibre optics and other forms of lighting into garments, they create clothing capable of generating spectacular effects. London-based photographer Atton Conrad created his own version of illuminated fashions by projecting swirling lights around models to create dresses he describes as 'light graffiti'.

OPPOSITE AND LEFT
This design from 2011 by Sweden-based Julia Krantz, dubbed Whiteness, covers the body in rigid panels that suggest robotic body parts more than traditional garments. Tube-like structures tracing the shoulders and torso suggest technological circuitry, while the overlapping panels appear ready to morph into new shapes.

even when the design and manufacture have concluded and the garment is worn on the body, clothing will respond to preprogrammed cues that enable it to refresh itself, to self-repair if damaged and even to download new tailoring templates in order to upgrade itself to the latest style. Garments will be designed with several stages of use in mind. An item of clothing that may appear to be a finished garment may in fact merely be at a stage in its evolution.

The way garments fit the body will be as important in the future as it is today, and fashion will feature anatomically inspired cuts that actively shape the body into an idealized form. Fabric panels will trace muscle groups and compress them to enhance their performance, boosting blood circulation and providing extra support to stimulate tired muscles and improve stamina and strength. Compression fabrics will press the body into an idealized shape, precluding the need for undergarments that support the wearer.

As surfaces change colourways, silhouettes shift and textures constantly transform, the next generation of fashion will emerge as a mutable media. Garments in their interstitial state may resemble gases, liquids and foams more than they do wearable technology. Classical tailoring will be replaced by innovative transformations, and transition will come to be a hallmark of fashion.

WEARABLE INTELLIGENCE

The way in which we get dressed will be radically different in the future. Nanoscience and self-replication technology can be applied to fashion as to other disciplines, indicating that self-assembly particles can form a garment if programmed to do so. London-based fashion designer Nancy Tilbury foresees a day when clothing will emerge from gas and active nanoparticles. One of Tilbury's research interests is what she terms 'body atmosphere', essentially a cloud of particles that will begin to assemble into a garment when it comes into contact with the wearer's body. These rapid-assembly particles could also be suspended in a liquid and applied in the manner of a lotion to the body, where they would bond together according to a preprogrammed fashion design. Such fashions would eliminate the need to shop for, try on and subsequently dress oneself in ready-made garments. Conventional packaging would disappear, and the wearer would no longer have to struggle with zips and fastenings.

Some clothing will be encoded with biological triggers, which will enable them to sense physiological changes and seasonal shifts, and to react to them: for example, by thickening in order to increase warmth, or by becoming more elastic when flexibility is required. Neri Oxman, a researcher at the Massachusetts Institute of Technology (MIT) Media Lab, studied medicine before taking an interdisciplinary approach to materials science. The varying behaviour of human bone (which becomes denser during pregnancy, for example, and thinner during travel in space), inspired Oxman to create composite walls that sense when to vary in density. Made of rubber, plastic and other materials,

BELOW, LEFT
Japanese manufacturer Kuchofuku produces 'air-conditioned clothing'. The fans, controls and power source are integrated into the clothes.

BELOW AND OPPOSITE
London-based fashion designer Nancy Tilbury believes that, in the future, the human body will be genetically engineered to make it possible for clothes and jewellery to grow on the surface of skin. She offers visions of how a ring could be 'grown' by the body rather than simply put on and worn (below), and foresees a day when clothing can be applied in lotion form (opposite). An interview with Nancy Tilbury and her partners at Studio XO appears on page 52.

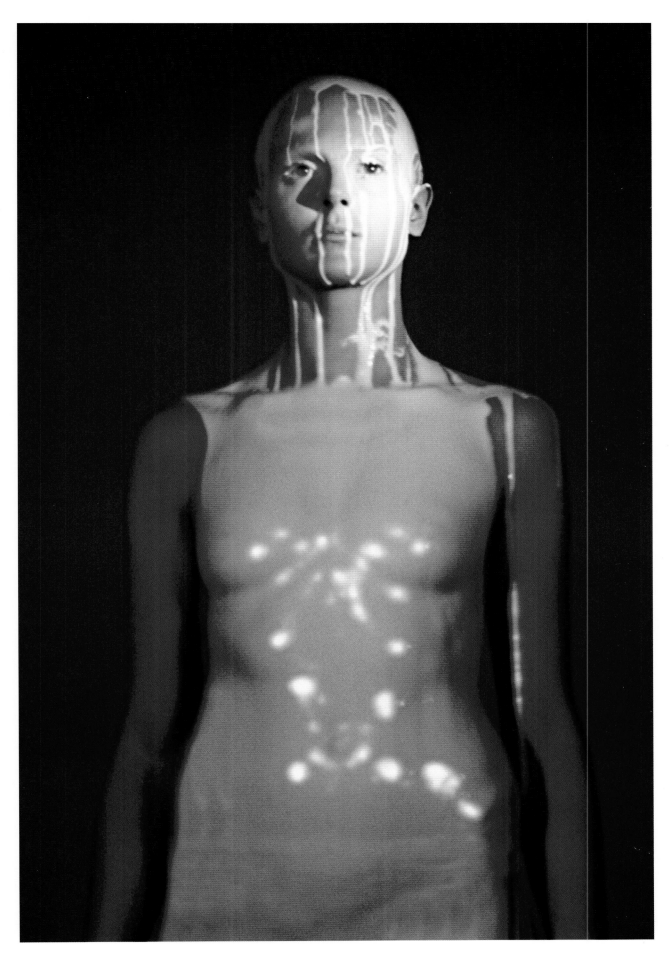

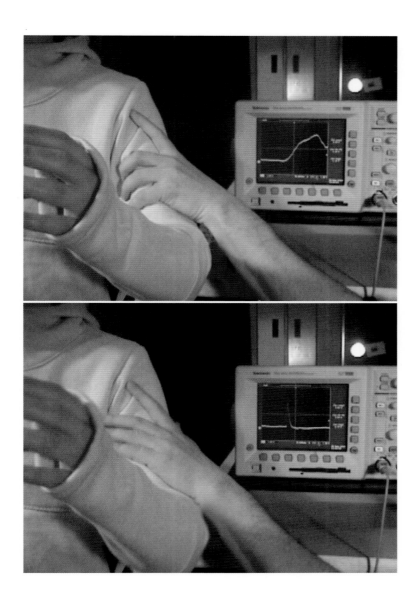

Many different types of technological system can be integrated into fashion. Soft circuits, conductive fibres and pressure-sensitive panels make it possible to create clothing that can react and respond to impact and force. Reseacher Adam Whiton and designer Yolita Nugent (see page 73) create items of clothing that sense contact and register the amount of force used. The prototype garments shown here could be worn by anyone wanting to thwart potential attackers.

OPPOSITE
Geometric shapes feature in many garments by the Russian fashion designer Irina Shaposhnikova, providing an alternative to the soft shapes and gentle contours characteristic of mainstream fashion. Such structured surfaces can easily conceal inelastic technological parts and position them comfortably on the body.

RIGHT
The boldly angular aesthetic of these shoes by Brazilian designer Andreia Chaves takes footwear in a new direction. New parameters for footwear will unfold in the future as shoes become fitted with, for example, devices that generate power.

the walls react to structural stress and such environmental factors as wind, automatically reconfiguring to form columns and create openings in the most structurally sound places.

Oxman's work includes body-hugging surfaces that react and reconfigure to each movement, and she has designed gloves that alleviate the pain of carpal tunnel syndrome by rigidifying as they sense the wearer making repetitive movements in the hand and wrist. Oxman anticipates a time when materials will have behaviours embedded within them. In fashion terms, such design technology will create fabric-like materials that endow garments with characteristics that make it appear as though they are 'thinking' for themselves.

One of the new 'behaviours' such garments will have is already within reach. Ludwik Leibler, a professor at the École supérieure de physique et de chimie industrielles (ESPCI) in Paris, has linked different groups of molecules together via hydrogen bonds. The molecules form the same kinds of chemical bond that hold water molecules together, creating a material with the texture and flexibility of rubber. In the same way as water does, the material has a remarkable ability to reconfigure and form new shapes. When the material breaks, the ends can be reattached to each other: when held together for fifteen minutes or so the edges will bond together again, effectively repairing the rupture. The material can be stretched to several times its length, making it ideal for garments where elasticity is required, such as socks, underwear and sports clothing. Made into a pair of tights, the material could repair itself if snagged and start to mend before tears had the chance to ladder.

The ultimate end to such technologically enhanced clothing would be for it to sense when it was no longer required and automatically disappear. British fashion designer Helen Storey is collaborating with scientist Tony Ryan to develop a fabric of water-soluble PVOH (polyvinyl alcohol; used, for example, in dissolvable laundry sachets). Garments made from the material would disintegrate when soaked in water, keeping obsolete garments out of landfill and eliminating the need to take them to a recycling unit. Storey came up with the concept in conjunction with a packaging design project, when she considered the concept of a shampoo bottle that disappears when the last drops are squeezed out. When applied to fashion, Storey's know-how would enable garments to self-destruct before the design and tailoring went out of style.

THE EXPERIENCE OF FASHION

Fashion is generally regarded as a known entity. Clothing is a tactile medium made for wear on the body, quantifiable when amassed in the wardrobe, and statistically measurable when considered in terms of production units, profit and loss. Yet fashion also mediates a wide range of subjective experiences that are less easy to quantify. The way clothing fits is open to interpretation by wearer and onlooker alike. Wearing a garment can open up a wide spectrum of emotions, which, in turn, provide gateways for a new range of experiences. Dress can be laden with emotions of anger, fear, sorrow, joy and optimism; it can make the body appear seductive, or desexualize the wearer altogether. Fashion takes us beyond the awareness of the garments lining our bodies and gives us a persona to assume when we wear it.

Future fashion will deliver more than a technological portal; garments will be inextricably intertwined with our experience of wearing them. Many fields of design are already exploring the attraction of multisensory products (that engage several of our senses, such as touch, sound and smell; see also interview with Charles Spence, page 126), examining how mood and emotion can motivate consumers to form positive associations with brand values. Cognitive scientists claim that clothing gives people a wider range of tactile experiences than non-wearable products, maintaining that fashion per se is suffused with more emotional signifiers and behavioural references than many other cultural forms. As the fashion industry moves forward, it will factor into clothing's design and end use greater emphasis on how clothes can be considered from cognitive and emotional perspectives. Future garments will be able to mimic cognitive abilities, such as intuition and logic, becoming compatible

with our moods and emotional triggers in order to make our experience of them more satisfying.

Emotions and the tactile senses are inextricably linked, and as a result fabrics' texture, surface and tactility are a significant part of the experience of wearing clothes. In years to come, haptic technology (technology that gives tactile feedback) will lead to a broader understanding of how the tactile senses might be embodied within a garment, enabling designers to amplify the sensory experience of clothing.

The exchange of glances between wearer and onlooker reveals much about a garment's impact on those who see it. Fashion researchers can apply eye-tracking technology, such as the systems created by NeuroFocus, a neuroscientific and neuromarketing company based in California, to see where onlookers direct their gaze and how their glance travels. Eye-tracking technology employs electroencephalography (the measurement and recording of electrical activity in different parts of the brain) to record brain activity, and measures skin responses to detect levels of arousal. These responses provide insights into an individual's subconscious feelings, emotions and subliminal reactions. NeuroFocus and other similar groups claim that their research methods enable them to access the subconscious desires that cannot be expressed by the consumer.

Gaining an understanding of the types of reaction clothing can generate gives designers a better understanding of how people think about fashion. Clothing is encountered through the senses, with touch and sight mediating the wearer's experience of a garment. Sensory stimuli, together with individual perceptions, preconceptions and spontaneous associations, activate a range of

Well-designed clothes can often be experienced in a variety of ways. The outfit shown here, from Haider Ackermann's Spring/Summer 2011 collection, may be regarded as being revealing, but its voluminous shape and generous cut also conceal the body.

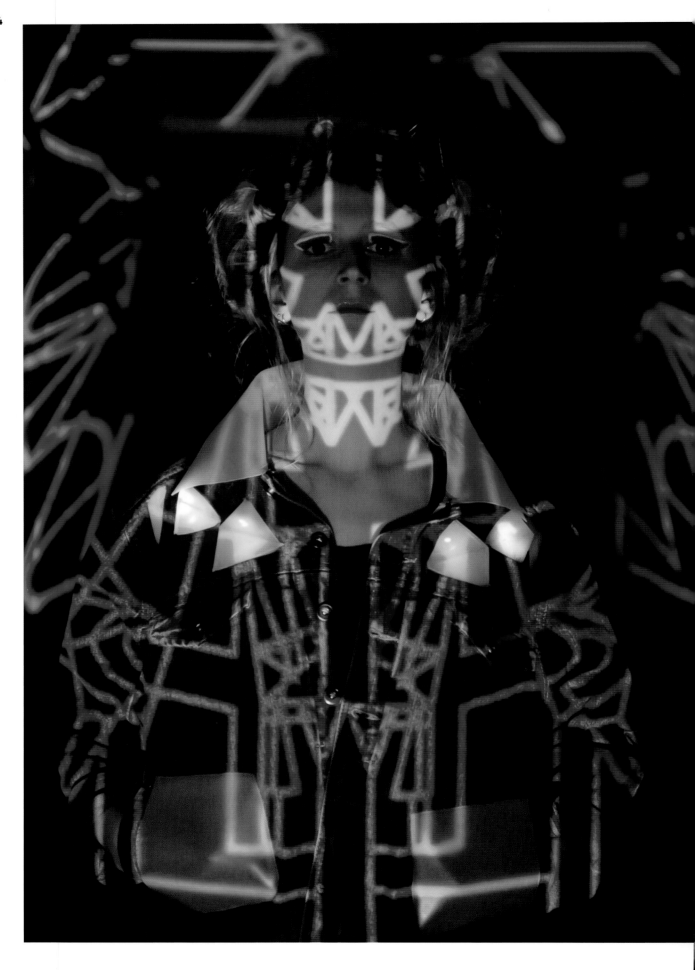

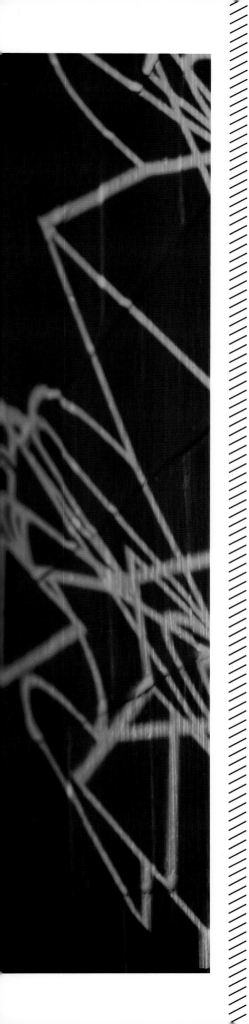

The Spike Jacket designed by Nancy Tilbury amplifies the wearer's perception of his or her personal space. The jacket's integrated technology system senses when other people come too close, prompting a system of textile cabling and silicone light diffusers to flash.

cognitive processes that spark our experiences. A wider awareness of what we wear, and others' responses to it, is gained through basic learning processes, decision-making mechanisms, high-level logic and planning. Such cognitive skills enable us to perceive an entire outfit even though we see only small parts of it at any one time; to imagine how a garment would look on ourselves or others; to remember earlier associations; and to project the way in which we experience fashion.

Fashion enables us to project a self-image and fosters a sense of belonging, and subsequently functions as a social tool that helps us to gain insights and form opinions about those around us. Such cognition is typically laden with emotion, motivating people to wear the clothing that makes them feel good and to shun those garments that elicit negative responses. Fashion consumers typically base their choice of clothing on what they want to communicate about themselves, and how they think their chosen outfit will be seen through the eyes of others.

Fashion's ability to communicate feelings is an area of interest to both designers and researchers, who are creating clothing that can detect emotions and broadcast them. Almost every type of emotion triggers a physiological response. Anger, for example, is typically accompanied by a hot flush and muscle tension; sadness often creates a feeling of tightness in the throat and tension in the lower abdomen; embarrassment can create hot flushes in the upper chest and face. Happiness is often accompanied by an expansive feeling as blood rushes to the chest, and induces relaxation in the arms and legs, while desire is often characterized by heavy breathing and an increased heart rate. Wearable diagnostic technology (see pages 81 and

221) can identify changes in heartbeat, respiration and perspiration, and spark preprogrammed changes in a garment's surface and shape in response.

As wearable systems identify bodily sensations and trigger responses, some emotions could be processed as a type of computation that translates an action. Philips Design, a research organization based in The Netherlands, was one of the first to combine wearable technology and sensory intelligence. Its Probes programme initiative developed such garments as the SKIN Bubelle, described as 'an exploration into emotional sensing': a dress designed with body sensors that could gauge the wearer's emotional state. The dress, launched in 2007, is created from bubble-like shapes that glow individually at an intensity related to the wearer's movements and changes in skin temperature. The effect creates a visual representation of the wearer's emotional state and physical responses.

Fashions endowed with the sensory capacity to identify and broadcast emotions heighten clothing's ability to say something about the wearer. Taking the technology a step further, designers have developed garments that enable the wearer to share emotions with another individual by sending a simulated embrace. London-based fashion laboratory CuteCircuit developed the Hug Shirt, a garment that can relay the experience of being hugged remotely through telecommunications technology. The shirt is embedded with sensors that are able to receive and transmit information from and to Java-enabled mobile phones. Hug Shirt-wearers can send virtual embraces to other wearers by touching sensorized areas on their own shirt, interacting with the fabric's surface as if it were a mouse pad in order to activate the pressure-

sensitive areas. The sensors monitor the pressure and duration of the hug, then relay it via wireless Bluetooth technology to another shirt, the wearer of which feels the embrace as the sensorized areas in his or her own shirt are triggered to mirror the movements and impressions made on the shirt that sent the hug.

In New York, Studio 5050, led by Despina Papadopoulos, designed a pair of jackets programmed to identify and respond to each other. The jackets are intended to facilitate social interaction, and, as in the unseen frisson of feeling between two individuals in love, they communicate through an invisible waveband spectrum. Pairs of these LoveJackets are engineered to emit a signal on a particular wave frequency, which they identify and track to find each other. As the jackets detect the signal, they respond by emitting bleeping noises, which are intended to mimic the cries made by mating crickets. The signal also triggers a pattern of LEDs (light-emitting diodes) on the jackets' surfaces to blink. The polling distance is short-range, requiring that the jackets come within 'sight' of each other to be detected. When the jackets are activated, the wearers should be close enough to see each other, enabling them to find their 'other half'. Studio 5050's subsequent HugJackets (2008) emit sound and light when a pair come together in an embrace.

As fashion breaks down boundaries between emotions and physical space, the messages garments convey about the wearer will be complex. Clothing may serve to provide metaphors for mental states, merging feeling and form into a single object. Whereas today garments tell us much about their wearer's external appearance, in future they may say more about the wearer's innermost feelings.

Developed as part of Philips Design's Probes programme, the SKIN Bubelle dress is constructed from bubble-like shapes that illuminate in response to the wearer's emotional state. As sensors in the base layer of the garment detect levels of arousal on the wearer's skin, they trigger microprojectors to emit light, enabling the dress to glow.

FASHION IN THE FIFTH DIMENSION

As cutting-edge fashion forges connections with modern science and technology, it is also beginning to align with physics and mathematics. Fashion's physical characteristics are easily quantified within the three spatial dimensions (length, breadth and depth), and also have resonance in the fourth dimension, time. Yet fashion has many other features that are less easy to quantify. For example, the sense of a garment's 'fit', the feelings induced by wearing clothing, the wearer's pursuit of self-expression and the satisfaction of dressing our bodies are familiar to all, but each interpretation is unique. These factors create the experience of fashion, an event horizon that is situated in time and space, yet has meanings that appear to transcend them.

Issey Miyake has long been a fashion innovator, and has continually challenged pre-existing explanations of fashion as he has explored new horizons. In the Reality Lab, a consortium he established in order to, as he put it, 'challenge, explore and celebrate the infinite possibilities of creativity', the Japanese designer identifies fresh insights into the meaning of clothing and charts new ways of thinking about it. The experience of fashion, in Miyake's thinking, begins the moment the garment is worn and communicates meanings to the wearer and onlooker. Miyake says that this is what brings the garment to life, and he describes the experience as the fifth dimension of fashion (in physics, the fifth dimension is a hypothetical dimension that would follow the fourth, time). Thinking of clothing in this way indicates that our interpretation of fashion cannot be quantified by time and space alone.

Miyake has a track record of putting his philosophical ideas to the test by translating them into physical forms. His concept of a fifth dimension was no exception, and he tasked the Reality Lab with realizing it. The Lab enlisted the help of Jun Mitani, a Japanese computer systems specialist who had designed a software program to construct three-dimensional geometric forms from a piece of paper. The result of the team's work was the '132 5' project (2010), the title of which explains the theory underpinning it: one piece of fabric (1), a three-dimensional shape (3) reduced to two dimensions (2) by folding, and the fifth dimension (5), being the experience of wearing it.

The 3D shapes of the garments designed for Miyake's '132 5' project were mathematically translated into two-dimensional geometry, from which patterns could be made. Instead of garments being made by cutting cloth and stitching it, lengths of fabric were folded according to the patterns and given sharp, precise creases that were permanently embedded in the cloth. In this folded, creased guise, the garments are merely flat forms hidden within geometric textures in cloth. When unfolded, and therefore expanded into their three-dimensional forms, they become complex, multi-faceted garments comprised of soft geometrical shapes. Visually, the garments appear to be natural extensions of Miyake's Pleats Please and A-POC (A Piece of Cloth) projects, which included pleated garments made from a single piece of cloth.

The '132 5' collection was launched at Galerie Kreo in Paris, where it was critically acclaimed by the art world and fashion press alike. In keeping with Miyake's intention that the garments should not be bound to time (there is no time in the fifth dimension, apparently), the collection is considered to be 'year-round', and therefore not attached to any particular season.

Bulgarian designer Amila Hrustic perceives fashion as a modular system. In her Plato collection of 2010, she created garments crafted with repeated identical geometric forms. On this dress the forms were set mostly on the right-hand side of the body to create an asymmetric configuration.

The Rick Owens Spring/Summer 2011 menswear collection was inspired by the idea of transcendence. The collection's sleek, clean lines and stark black-and-white colour palette suggest Zen-like simplicity, while the asymmetrical cuts, irregular panels and oversized collars take men's clothing in a fresh direction.

SENSORY SURFACES

If a garment is an extension of the body, then its surface is an extension of the skin. Fashioned skins, whether made of leather, fur, natural fibres, metal fibres or synthetic materials, are surfaces loaded with meaning. Fashion surfaces can be multilayered and multidimensional, and be designed to invite the gaze or to deflect it. They can be so richly decorated that they draw the eye closer, or, as can be the case with fetish wear, for example, embellished with textures so repellent that onlookers recoil in fear.

With the advent of wearable technology, fashion surfaces are revealing their potential to do more than simply decorate the clothing they cover. They are becoming information hubs capable of gathering data from the environment around them, and able to exchange data with other technological systems. Embellished with sensors and electroluminescent wires, garments can detect ambient sound and light around them. By interconnecting sound-recognition sensors, optic sensors and microcontrollers, surfaces are able to respond to noise and light and to display their responses on their surface. Clothing can also react to fluctuations in ambient temperature.

In the future, digital media and light-emitting fibres will embellish almost all fashion surfaces. Colourful patterns of LEDs can project computer graphic applications, illuminating the surface of a garment and reconfiguring into a range of motifs. One of the most revolutionary digital media surfaces to date was created in 2008 by British fashion designer Hussein Chalayan in collaboration with London-based interactive design expert Moritz Waldemeyer, in the form of dresses capable of projecting moving images. The front of each dress featured an electronic-screen-like surface created by 15,600 LEDs and Swarovski crystals embroidered in the fabric. On one dress, a looped film showed a time-lapse sequence of a rose beginning to bloom, while another dress screened images of sharks swimming in a frothy sea.

Chalayan and Waldemeyer later teamed up again to create dresses that projected laser beams across their surfaces. Waldemeyer assembled hundreds of motor-driven laser diodes and integrated them into the garments; each diode was able to rotate in several directions. The laser diodes were paired with Swarovski crystals, positioned either to deflect the lasers or to absorb their light, depending on the angle of the beam. When the lasers were beamed directly into the crystals, they made the crystals glow. When the beams were deflected, they travelled far beyond the surface of the garment into the surrounding space. The resulting spectacle created a burst of moving lights that transformed the surfaces into constantly changing animated screens. As the laser beams projected beyond the dress's surface, they extended the boundaries of its silhouette, making it seem borderless, even ethereal. The boundaries between fabric and the space surrounding it became blurred, making the wearer appear to be cocooned in a starburst of radiating lights rather than a dress.

Eunjeong Jeon's Trans-For-M-otion designs (see page 47) detect the body's movement and interact with the wearer as he or she moves. The garment's sensory capacity and kinetic properties enable it to change shape in order to make the wearer more comfortable. LEDs intended to soothe the wearer can be integrated into the garment. Coloured lights promote relaxation, calming the wearer during stressful situations. Bright white lights enhance the wearer's vision in darkness, and make the person more visible.

SHIFTING SILHOUETTES

There is more to fashion fabrics than their simply being a façade; they are chosen for their capacity to disguise the garment's construction and their aptitude for moulding naturally to the wearer's physique. A dress can sit close to the body's contours and emphasize its natural shape, or be worn with corsetry, bustiers and padding to sculpt the body into an idealized form. Some fashions disguise the body altogether, using rigid materials to redefine it radically, or to cocoon the body in garments with architecture-like proportions.

Historically, women of fashion have always been somewhat hidden. Padded at the shoulders, bust and hips, and 'enhanced' through layers of fabric, high collars and flowing skirts, they were characterized more by the shape of their silhouette than by individual garments. The androgynous styles of the 1960s changed everything, removing the wasp-like silhouette from fashion, and the body consciousness of the 1980s introduced a vogue for sculpting the physique through fitness and exercise rather than through clothing. Shoulder pads and push-up bras became fashion fixtures again towards the end of the 1980s, and designers recommenced flirting with corsetry and bustiers in the 1990s. Since then, mainstream fashion has been characterized more by relatively loose-fitting garments than by ones that sculpt the body into an idealized form.

Such unstructured designs, including voluminous skirts, draped dresses and oversized tops, are cut to fit a broad range of body types, and their manufacture does not require the complicated pattern-cutting and labour-intensive production processes of sleeker designs. As this considerably streamlines production processes, it reduces costs and makes it more profitable for fashion companies to produce shapeless silhouettes than streamlined ones.

In recent years, leading designers have revived interest in form-fitting styles and dramatic silhouettes. Crisp shapes, military-inspired designs and the popularity of vintage clothing have inspired sleeker proportions and have placed more emphasis on tailoring: the body is elongated through the use of tall silhouettes that make the waist appear higher and the legs seem longer, while an element of efficiency is introduced by layered tiers and robust, almost athletic tailoring and trim borrowed from menswear. New types of fastening system are being developed to heighten transformability and adaptability, which will make it easier to store and transport garments that create voluminous silhouettes.

New, lightweight materials are introducing the notion of weightless volume. Fabrics that are stiff yet flexible make it possible to create large silhouettes without compromising wearability or manufacturing techniques. Volume expands the range of the garment around the wearer, amplifying its impact and effect. Bell-shaped skirts, full sleeves, swing hems and large collars that frame the face can make a strong fashion statement, while designs that envelop the wearer in billowing shapes and gentle textures soften the silhouette. A vogue that will continue into the future was started by the soft origami-inspired garments crafted by such designers as Rei Kawakubo and Junya Watanabe for Autumn/Winter 2000–01: their clothes created complex silhouettes that combined geometric lines with organic textures.

New computer-aided design tools, algorithmic modelling and mathematical software scripts make it easier to design layered structures, to fold flat planes and to create unusual angles that craft strikingly geometric silhouettes, generating

Iris van Herpen's designs are characterized by contours that accentuate parts of the body not normally highlighted by conventional garments. This top, from her Escapism collection of Autumn/Winter 2011–12, embellishes the collarbone, creating a silhouette that emphasizes the top of the chest.

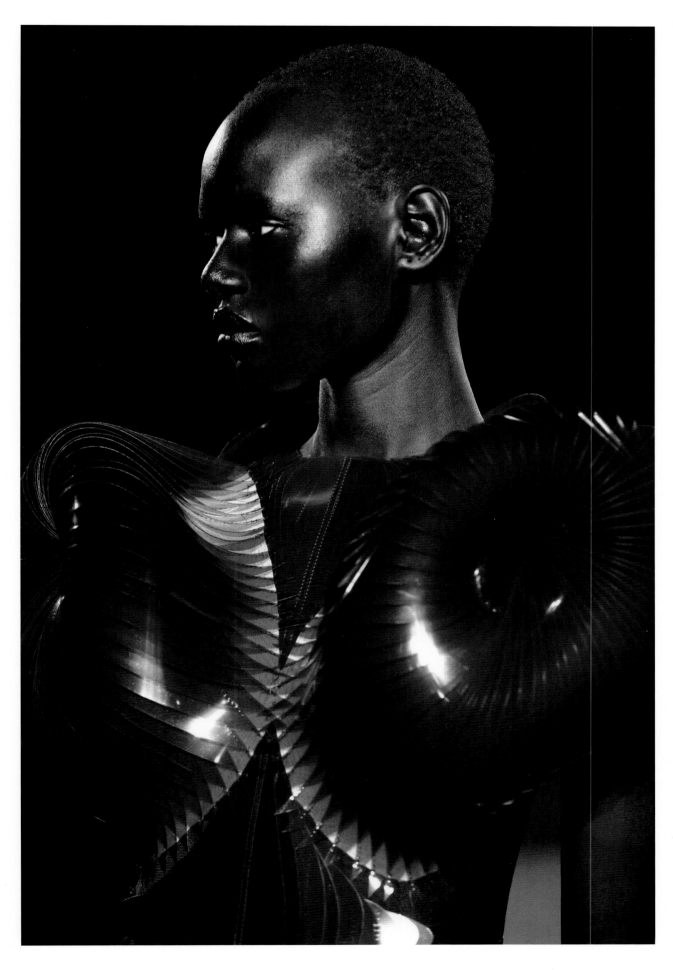

fragmented shapes that create angular surfaces and bold lines around the body. Such styles are inspiring today's designers and are establishing a fresh direction for the fashion silhouettes of the future. Moscow-based designer Irina Shaposhnikova contributed to the look with her inspirational Crystallographica collection of 2009, which consisted of garments with strong geometric forms and sharp facets (opposite). The garments were crafted in cotton, wool and silk organza fused with synthetic materials that emphasized their bold outlines.

Bulgarian designer Amila Hrustic also explored the potential of creating a strictly geometric silhouette in her Plato collection of 2010 (pages 48–49). By tracing the body's natural outline in geometric shapes, Hrustic forged a dialogue between mathematical forms and organic contours. The two complement each other; as the body moves, light highlights the polyhedral shapes and transforms the surface into a field of 3D geometric shapes that gives the wearer an unexpectedly crisp silhouette.

Balkan designer Alice Zixxheddu has derived inspiration from the geometry of nature, creating a fashion collection of what she calls 'living clothes' that replicate refractive forms she has observed in mineral crystals and glaciers. Zixxheddu used 3D software to translate these shapes into garments, amplifying and distorting the geometry to achieve dramatic textures and volumes, and incorporating light sensors into the clothes to trigger changes

of shape to the surfaces. Combined with memory materials and activated by wireless technology, areas of the surfaces fold and unfold in response to changes in ambient light, altering the garment's silhouette.

Australia-based designer and researcher Eunjeong Jeon is bringing natural fibres and technology together in her PhD work to create Transe-For-M-otion, a kinetic garment that morphs into new silhouettes. The garment is crafted from felted wool embedded with wearable technology. Sensors monitor muscle tension, breathing, heart rate and temperature to detect when the wearer experiences discomfort. The garment reacts automatically by closing around the wearer to foster a greater sense of security. As a result, the shape of the silhouette relates directly to wearers' sense of emotional and physical well-being, literally enabling them to wear their heart on their sleeve.

The technologically enhanced garments being developed today have complex surfaces, relying on texture, embellishment and reactive surfaces to conceal embedded mechanics and devices. They necessitate silhouettes that are capable of morphing into new shapes and then regaining their original profile, yet that are strong enough to temper stark geometric outlines and striking enough to flatter the wearer. In the future, silhouettes will do more than shape the body; they will provide a dynamic means of interacting with the spaces surrounding them.

IRIS VAN HERPEN

Dutch designer Iris van Herpen, who is known for her sculptural silhouettes and pioneering use of digital technology, started her own label in 2007 following a stint at Alexander McQueen. Her work proposes fresh directions for fashion, combining traditional tailoring techniques with new materials and innovative construction processes. Van Herpen used 3D printing technology to design and fabricate her Escapism collection (Autumn/Winter 2011–12), which brought her critical acclaim and cemented her reputation as a visionary designer. The silhouettes she creates bring texture, structure and materials together in a new guise, giving the female form an otherworldly appearance. Although Van Herpen takes garments to aesthetic extremes, each of her designs is underpinned by a futuristic vision of beauty and a determination to make artistic expression the basis of all she creates. When interviewed for this book, she pointed out that future aesthetics should reflect individual creativity rather than function or commercial trends. That said, Van Herpen is not striving to create 'futuristic' designs; she regards her work as being timeless.

How are new materials creating fresh directions for fashion?

Exploring new processes and new materials enables fashion to move forward. For example, my Escapism collection emerged as the result of seeing what the possibilities of using 3D printing within fashion would be. The 3D-printed dresses I designed were not intended for everyday wear, simply because the material they are made from is fragile. 3D printing technology has advanced since then, making it possible to print clothing in flexible thin rubbers. I think it is only a matter of time before it will be possible to 3D-print washable fabrics, and after that, there will be a huge shift in fashion. The sewing machine will quickly become redundant, and the ways in which designers think and create will change too.

What will the silhouettes of the future look like?

There will always be a lot of different styles in fashion, just as there are today. There are likely to be big differences between people as well, so I doubt there will be any one, uniform silhouette. One hundred years ago, people could not conceive of the digital world we live in today, and I think that fashion, one hundred years from now, will be equally impossible to predict.

In what ways is technology influencing your work?

Technology creates new design possibilities and innovative materials. It brings me the opportunity to collaborate with architects and other design companies. Yet new technology also brings new limitations, because every technique and material has its own restrictions.

Possibilities and limitations are always a big part of creating a new design.

When I experimented with 3D printing, my ways of designing changed radically. The drawings of the 3D-printed dresses had to be translated into millimetre details in the computer, forcing me to use a technologized process that is the opposite of drawing and pattern-cutting freehand. I find it hard to control the design process so strictly, but at the same time, it challenges me and brings me new ways of seeing things and new ways of thinking about design.

'Weightless volume' is considered to be a hallmark of the fashions to come. Is it already emerging today?

I don't work with weightlessness myself, or particularly aim to create it, but many of my newer pieces are quite lightweight and create volume around the body. This is especially apparent in recent collections. The 3D-printed garments are not heavy at all, thanks to the lightweight polyamide materials they are made from, and they may be considered 'weightless' in comparison with other types of clothing.

What innovations would you like to see in future fashions?

I hope designers will be able to manipulate materials more efficiently than we can today, and that there will be a totally new generation of 'super' materials that do not exist today. Apart from that, it would be a good thing if fashion actually becomes non-material. Future fashions could include ways to dress in substances that are not touchable or stable, but actually move and change with the wearers'

moods and expressions. Rather than wearing clothes made out of solid substances, in future people could be dressed in such things as smoke, drops of water, coloured vapour or radio waves. Clothes could have the same body language as the wearer, moving with the body rather than restricting it.

Van Herpen's Crystallization collection (Spring/Summer 2011; top right) was the first in which she showed garments made with 3D printing technology, for which she teamed up with architect Daniel Widrig and digital manufacturer .MGX. She continued the association for her Escapism collection (Autumn/Winter 2011–12; top left and bottom row). Despite their volume and mass, the pieces are remarkably light, and their sleek symmetry shows the precision with which 3D-printed garments can be produced.

STUDIO XO

Since fashion designer Nancy Tilbury, couture craftsman Ian Wallace and designer and engineer Benjamin Males teamed up as Studio XO in order to pool their talents, they have created some of the most technologically advanced clothing worn today. From its lab in London, Studio XO created stage costumes for the Black Eyed Peas' world tour in 2011; these costumes were among the first to have 'connectivity', enabling them to communicate directly with wireless systems in and around the stage, and, potentially, even members of the audience. Whereas commissions to design interactive garments that could play video, trigger audio loops and project light shows would have challenged most designers, Tilbury, Wallace and Males hit back with well-considered, highly imaginative, technologically advanced designs that projected and amplified the movements choreographed by the performers. As the three describe their work and their philosophy here in a single voice, they channel the fashion of the future, telling us to expect 'a phase of physical and digital intimacy'.

What makes Studio XO unique within fashion design?

Whereas historically, technology and engineering have been kept separate from design and the creative world, we actively promote collaborations between them.

At Studio XO we work in a completely integrated way with the engineers, scientists, designers and craftspeople contributing at every stage, from conception to execution. To enable this kind of collaboration, the members of our teams have to exhibit a unique way of thinking and creating in order to allow them to operate in the 'grey' space, the crossover area in the fields of art, design and engineering that we call hybrid design.

What directions will fashion take in the future?

We believe that technology is enabling fashion design to move closer to a magical 'amalgam' area. Practitioners will seek to gain the technological skills necessary to operate within it, and a new platform for fashion will be established.

Changes will be seen in the way in which engineering and design are taught in colleges and universities, and also in the way in which companies deal with fashion. The cycle of fashion will be rejuvenated by these new hybrid practitioners, who will value heritage and craft, use rapid-manufacture techniques, and reform digital and physical retail. The entire architecture of fashion will be transformed.

Our relationship with clothing and its active and emotional output will modify our connection to fashion as we know it today.

Your stage costumes can exchange information wirelessly with lighting, video and audio relays on stage. Is there potential for other types of garment to do the same?

With the rapid growth of Wi-Fi and 3G networks we see a clear connection between intelligent garments and the internet. A perhaps obvious and clearly significant role for garments that can 'talk' to the world will be in the medical arena, where diagnostic clothes could update doctors with patients' vital signs, or in the military, where intelligent fatigues could, for example, publish a status report on the entry conditions of bullets or shrapnel and therefore better diagnose the damage done.

How could integrated lighting transform everyday fashions?

Creating garments that can illuminate certain areas on the body and display static and animated images will drastically change the way in which we consider clothing. By crafting lighting systems into the seams and darts of our clothing, we could disguise the areas of the body we want to conceal and highlight the ergonomics of the body to emphasize what we consider to be our 'best bits'.

Are these garments likely to last longer than conventional clothing?

The look and feel of our clothing would be reconfigured by dynamic lighting, intimate sensing and even physical adaptations to the surface and underlying structure of the garments. We hope technology-embedded body architectures will transform our appreciation of fashion, making us less likely to throw garments away after just a few

Studio XO created striking performance costumes for the 2011 world tour of alternative hip-hop band the Black Eyed Peas. Suits were fitted with LED modules (above) and transparent silicon studs underpinned with a network of LEDs (opposite), enabling them to function as graphic spectrum analysers that blinked and pulsed to the music.

The Black Eyed Peas are known for pushing the boundaries of music, and the custom-made, technologically enhanced illuminating performance costumes created for the band by Studio XO challenged the boundaries of fashion and technology as well.

seasons. We would keep a piece of light- and video-enhanced clothing for a lot longer, as the surface of the textile can be reprogrammed from season to season, maintaining the aesthetic value of the piece. Technology may well play a vital role in sustaining our relationship with fashion, altering the current status of so-called 'throw-away chic'.

What innovations would you like to see in the fashions of the future?

We would like to see every garment equipped with a multitude of sensing and computation abilities that connect wearers to social-media platforms, their home, family members, colleagues and so on. Such garments will provide ways to enhance us as humans, bringing to light a new world of fashion and couture experiences. This is already happening in the forms of 3D-printed clothing, digital look books and fashion with integrated networked technology.

However, we would like to see more radical changes, such as the dress Nancy conceived, which emerges after an individual has swallowed a tablet as it triggers a skin response that enables a textile layer to form around the pores of that person's skin. Another of Nancy's designs, the 'Cloud' gown, which is created by microrobots deployed to float around the human body and form a garment, would make a textile layer redundant altogether. We would also like to see skin systems transform, so that technologists could physically farm couture skins on the surface of our bodies, creating sculpted skin architectures, such as skin-and-bone eyebrows, organic stiletto heels, skin drapes and jewellery.

POWER
PERFOR

URBAN CAMOUFLAGE
BIO-PROTECTION
FUTURE FORCE
SPORTSWEAR
SUPERHUMAN STYLE

Interviews with
MARIA JANSSEN
SARAH BRADDOCK CLARKE

AND
MANCE

A new generation of second-skin apparel, protective clothing and high-performance sportswear is on the horizon, inspired by surprising sources, ranging from materials innovation to nature's own processes

Future fashion will be minimal in look, but maximal in performance. Many of us are always on the go, commuting and travelling, and this 'nomadic' aspect of twenty-first-century life has an impact on our expectations and demands of clothing: urban fashions will evolve to accommodate the need for refuge and protection within the city. Thanks to the proliferation of modern security and safety systems, humans may statistically be safer now than ever before, but perceptions of rising crime, inner-city violence and the threat of terrorism make protection a key concern. Scientists and researchers are developing textiles and devices that create protective clothing for a range of applications, and many of these innovations have the potential to form part of the wardrobe of the future.

Our capacity to withstand danger is being dramatically enhanced by a new generation of second-skin apparel, protective clothing and high-performance sportswear. These will be inspired by surprising sources, ranging from materials innovation to nature's own processes. Garments made for military applications enable soldiers to stand their ground in the face of attack and to use stealth to proceed undetected. Sportswear is taking athletes to new heights, and advances in aerodynamic surfaces enable runners, skiers and skaters to achieve record-breaking speeds. Thanks to fibres that bond in alignment with muscle groups, 'superhuman' styles of sportswear work with the body to give the wearer added strength, or rigidify around it to create garments invulnerable to assault. These and other innovations pave the way for future fashions to be crafted from shock- and impact-resistant materials, creating near-weightless designs that provide unprecedented comfort and protection.

As individual garments begin acquiring a new range of capabilities, multifunctionality will become the norm. Wearers will be able to perform a wider range of activities as a result, and the shift will be significant. Future designs will be divided into clothing that is either passive or active, according to the range of functionalities it affords the wearer. The sections that follow chart the materials, systems, technologies and designs that can endow everyday clothing with previously unimaginable resilience and strength.

OPPOSITE
Dutch designer Tim Smit created this 'Urban Security Suit' to insulate the wearer against pollution, airborne toxins and poisonous gases. The garment is made with a neoprene shell for insulation and shock protection, and is lined with body-moulded slashproof Kevlar that protects the wearer from attack.

PAGES 60–61
Australia's Cathy Freeman starts her winning run in the women's 400 metres at the 2000 Summer Olympics in Sydney. The Nike Swift Suit she was wearing, introduced that year (see also page 78), dramatically reduces drag, considerably boosting the athlete's performance. The Swift Suit technology has had impact in mainstream sportswear, inspiring a new breed of lightweight, aerodynamic training clothes for amateur athletes and fitness enthusiasts.

URBAN CAMOUFLAGE

As digital media enable the surfaces of garments to reconfigure (see Sensory Surfaces, page 42), they can also camouflage people wearing these clothes as they move through different terrains. Magnetic fields and electrical currents can create new textures in preprogrammed fabrics by causing them to rotate, ripple or form new configurations. Robert Langer, a chemical engineer and nanotechnologist based at MIT's Institute for Soldier Nanotechnologies, observed that the colours of conductive fibres could be controlled by an electrical impulse. By manipulating the power frequency, new colourways can be created. Langer is using the technology as the basis for developing a colour-changing textile that will camouflage soldiers, and this has the potential to be applied to fashion garments to make their surfaces changeable.

New materials technology may also make it possible for garments – and wearers – to disappear altogether. Research into optical camouflage, a means of disguise in which surfaces change colour or luminosity in order to blend in with their surroundings, has sparked the development of active camouflage technologies, materials and coatings. Active camouflage systems are highly technologically advanced, relying on wearable wireless technologies similar to those being developed for fashion garments.

Scientist Susumu Tachi, the founding president of the Virtual Reality Society of Japan, used similar technology to create the 'invisibility cloak'. The garment, which resembles an ordinary hooded overcoat but is made of a retro-reflective fabric in which the surface acts as a photographic screen, is linked to a camera recording the scenes behind it. The images are projected on to the front of the garment, effectively rendering it and the wearer transparent as those facing them, or looking at them through a viewfinder, see the scenery that would normally be blocked from view. The impression is created that the cloak and its wearer are not there at all.

The technology behind Tachi's invisibility cloak has resonance within the emerging field of 'illusion wear', in which researchers are manipulating garment surfaces to create the illusion of silhouettes not normally viable in clothing design. By using the garment's surface as a screen, researchers are striving to make the wearer appear slimmer, more toned or more voluptuous. Illusion-wear surfaces could mimic the appearance and texture of a wide range of materials, such as fur and snakeskin, reproduce motifs or create a range of different colours on the surface of the garment.

The value of Tachi's technology to the fields of defence, security and health care is potentially considerable. Tachi claims that the system could be applied to surgical gloves, which would film from the palm and project the images on to the back of the hand. Effectively, it would render surgeons' hands 'invisible', so that they could see areas of the patient's body that are normally obscured when probing the wound and handling surgical tools. Improving a surgeon's ability to see while performing a surgical procedure increases the likelihood of it being a complete success.

Natural invisibility occurs when a surface neither reflects nor absorbs light – that is, light has been able to pass through the object. Surfaces, and therefore objects, are visible only because light is reflected off them and travels to the viewer's eye. Natural surfaces that allow light to pass through them, none of which are transparent enough to be

OPPOSITE AND PAGE 64
Nancy Tilbury's Digital Skins series explores the extent to which textiles could be programmed to create changeable patterns, in the manner of the varying tones and colours of a chameleon's skin, and be engineered to merge into the background in order to make the wearer seem invisible.

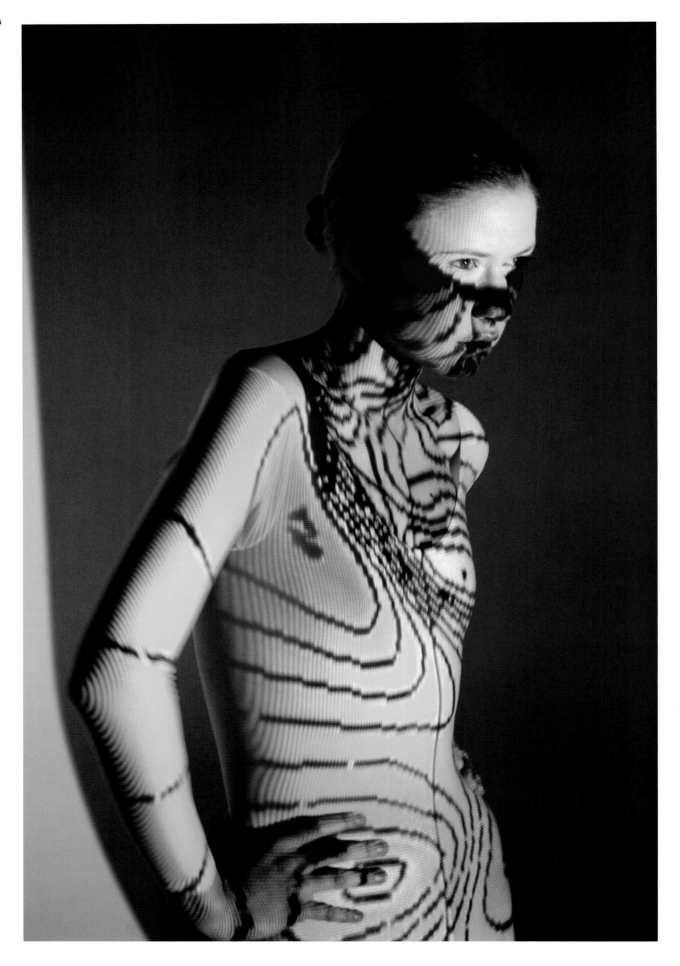

From Nancy Tilbury's Digital Skins series; see caption on page 62.

truly invisible, are described as translucent. Although the laws of science dictate that no object can be rendered completely invisible, the development of materials that can deflect light waves enables objects to be cloaked temporarily. If scientists are able to create surfaces that allow light waves to pass around them, there would be no visible trace of the objects these surfaces conceal. Such materials would, in theory, manipulate the relationship between light and mass to the degree that the object covered in them would not even cast a shadow.

With the challenge of creating invisibility in mind, a research team led by Xiang Zhang, a professor at the University of California, Berkeley, is engineering materials at the nanoscale level in order to create surfaces that redirect light waves around them, as well as sound and radio waves. Zhang and his team have created fabric-like meshes of nanoscale strands of silver fluoride and magnesium fluoride, and nanowires crafted from silver particles. These surfaces have the ability to curve light waves completely around the object they conceal so that, effectively, light flows past it, just as a stream of water would flow around a stone.

Sir John Pendry, a professor at Imperial College, London, led a similar research initiative. He developed a surface that engages microwave beams heading towards it and 'bends' them in order to make them flow smoothly past. Such surfaces would not be limited to manipulating microwave beams, but would also bend magnetic fields and light and radio waves. Not only would garments made with these surfaces appear invisible within most wave spectrums, but they would also cloak any technology embedded within them and render it undetectable.

As new technologies heighten clothing's potential to create devices for observation and stealth, they also transform clothes into vehicles for self-expression. Whereas a garment's surface has traditionally communicated something about the wearer's sense of chic, such innovations would probably say as much about individuals' technological aptitude as they would about sartorial style.

BIO-PROTECTION

Protective clothing aims to provide safety and security, which are among the most primal human needs. Clothing can compensate for the vulnerability of the body, providing practical solutions to the risks to urban cyclists, for example, who face the threat of collisions with vehicles and of injuries resulting from falling off their bicycle. Some pedestrians foray into areas gripped by violence and crime, where they face the danger of physical assault or even attack by feral dogs. To take this to extremes, civilian staff working in conflict zones may be subjected to sniper fire or airborne projectiles.

Garments are currently made to meet these needs, but most have more in common with the heavy body armour worn by medieval knights than with contemporary street style. Rather than being items of clothing, ancient armour encased warriors within surfaces more akin to the hard shells of crustaceans. These rigid forms moved with the wearer, mimicking the tough exoskeletons (rigid external covering) of insects, yet the weight of the metal restricted movement and hindered the wearer in combat. Today, designers creating protective garments strive to create surfaces with the resilience of armour and the flexibility of fabric. While metallic fibres, tough polymeric materials (made from molecules or other small units bonded together) and padded surfaces can be used to shield the body, they are often so tough that they create the experience of fortified fashion rather than clothing that can be worn comfortably.

According to Janine Benyus, co-founder of the Biomimicry 3.8 group, based in Montana, protective clothing could be more comfortable and efficient if it were inspired by the natural world. Benyus advocates the use of biomimetic design, which employs synthetic methods that mimic

biomechanical processes, believing that, because the need for protection is driven by instinct, nature's own solutions are the best means of soothing human fears and fostering a sense of security. 'Think about how warning colours, such as yellow and black, and red and black, get our attention', she said in a telephone interview for this book. 'They are subconscious reminders of killer wasps and poisonous coral snakes, things that early humans wanted to steer clear of, and they continue to trigger our fight-or-flight response today.'

While humans have evolved with the capacity to outrun danger, some other life forms have developed the means to ward off predators by staying put. The sea cucumber, for example, is a jelly-like marine organism whose body mass consists mostly of collagen fibres. 'The organism holds its own when threatened', Benyus explained. 'Its fibres cross-link and bond, enabling it to become rock-hard and remain so until the predator moves on. If phase-change fibres in kneepads could cross-link similarly upon impact, yet reverse and become soft again, they could protect the wearer without creating lasting bulk around the knees.'

Benyus points out that insect exoskeletons provide a viable template for many types of protective wear. Such lightweight, resilient synthetic fabrics as Kevlar, Twaron and Aracon (see page 110) are slash-proof and strong enough to withstand the grip of canine teeth. Made into garments, they line the body with a tough surface that moves with the wearer, much in the manner of the shells of crickets and grasshoppers. 'Insects and arthropods also have hair-like external sensors that monitor the air-flow field over their bodies', Benyus said. 'They detect pressure changes and vibrations emanating from a predator. Understanding these

OPPOSITE
Soft, pliable motorcycle racing suits, such as this one from Japanese performance sportswear label Hyod, act as a supple exoskeleton around the body. In the manner of insects' shells, these types of garment form a protective membrane around the wearer that moves with the body.

PAGES 68–69
The Hövding collar is a shape-shifting fashion accessory that can make a critical difference. Swedish company Hövding took airbag technology and concealed it in a stand-alone 'collar' that deploys on impact to form a helmet around the wearer's head. The deployment mechanism is activated by sensors that detect movements characteristic of a cyclist falling off a bicycle. Practical and ergonomic and unisex, Hövding's helmet complies with current Swedish bicycle safety regulations.

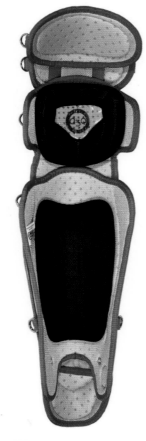

OPPOSITE
The Performance DH ski race suit by Spyder, founded in 1978 by Canadian competitive skier David Jacobs, is ergonomically designed to fit close to the skier's body and move with it. Compression keeps the suit close to the body, making it fit like a second skin, while the position of the seams reduces drag when the skier is racing downhill.

LEFT
Biomimetic approaches to performance apparel, together with new, flexible materials, have resulted in shin guards that perform with the same flexibility as human joints. This baseball shin guard (views show the inside and the outside) by the American company All-Star is designed with features that make it durable and lightweight, as well as comfortable.

complex sensory systems will enable designers to re-create them in garment form, where they can alert the wearer to potential threats.' Such surfaces could be engineered to emit biosonar (echolocation) signals similar to those of dolphins and bats, using echolocation as an anti-collision device that would help the wearer to avoid approaching traffic.

Benyus claims that the ability of some plants and animals to create changes on their surface could inspire the production of garments with the capacity to ward off attackers as soon as they sense physical contact. For example, the bioluminescence of the firefly, which secretes chemicals in order to emit light, can be reproduced in fabric form. According to Benyus, 'Bioluminescence in insects attracts mates or prey, but when re-created in clothing it could project light towards a human attacker, effectively placing them under a spotlight that they would want to run away from.'

Surfaces that detach altogether provide an effective means of eliminating predators, as Benyus notes. 'The eucalyptus tree has scaly bark that it drops when it has the weight of vines on it. As the tree releases the bark, the vines fall off.' If this system were applied to garments, surfaces that stick to an attacker and detach from the wearer could hinder the attacker long enough for the wearer to get away. Certain species of lizard, such as geckos and most types of skink, will sacrifice their tail in order to escape predators. The wildly wagging tail will attract the predator's attention, and when the predator pounces on the appendage the tail detaches itself from the lizard's body, while the vulnerable head and torso escape (the tail will generally grow back over time). If this concept were applied to fashion, garments could, for example, deploy a decoy handbag while concealing the wearer's

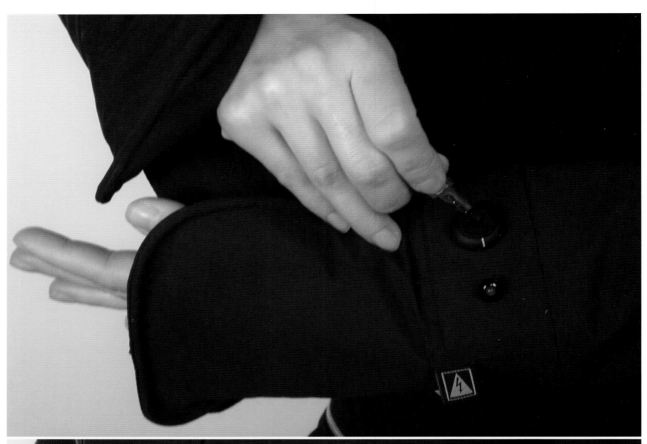

valuables within a hidden inner layer, or quickly manifest dummy mobile phones or laptops to mislead a would-be robber.

Other species of lizard, such as the Eastern skink, which is native to the deserts of the Arabian Peninsula, are thought to create electric charges along their scales that repel sand grains. Adam Whiton and Yolita Nugent, researchers based at the Massachusetts Institute of Technology (MIT), used this approach in 2003 to create a protective layer for the human body. Using the pressure-sensitive conductive materials known as quantum tunnelling composites (QTCs; see page 119), Whiton and Nugent developed the No-Contact jacket (opposite), in which the outer surface deploys an electrical charge when grabbed, gripped or constricted.

In nature, slippery surfaces can also be effective in thwarting predators. Benyus offers the example of the hagfish, an elongated eel-like creature capable of secreting copious amounts of slime when threatened. 'The fish releases dry granules that transform into slime as they absorb the water around them. It makes the fish too slippery for predators to get hold of, and can even conceal the fish within a thick coating of slime.' Translated into fashion, this idea could be applied to a garment's surface, so that an attacker would be prevented from getting a firm grip on the wearer.

Some aquatic creatures suck in water or air when threatened, dramatically increasing their size. In porcupine fish, for example, the sharp spines that normally lie against their bodies pop up and radiate outwards as a result, making them appear threatening to predators. Land-bound organisms can also use liquid to augment muscle strength and improve their ability to escape predators. Cicadas, for example, rarely fly; but they are able to flee from danger when required thanks to a superficial system of veins that deploys their wings by pumping fluid through them.

The Italian materials and technology research laboratory Grado Zero Espace has created a 'hydroskeleton' suit for use by astronauts making spacewalks. The system pumps aerogel around the body to cool astronauts as they face high solar temperatures. Grado Zero Espace redesigned the astronaut's hydroskeleton for a protective garment intended for firefighters and steel workers (the Hydro jacket), and later adapted the system for high-performance fashion jackets.

As biomimicry becomes established as a field of innovation and inspiration, and as biomimetic design spurs a wider understanding of nature's protective processes, potent solutions are being developed to create protective garments and performance wear.

FUTURE FORCE

Military-style clothing is popular among civilians today. Combat trousers, military tailoring and camouflage prints feature on fashion catwalks around the world. Although army-surplus garments and military footwear are staples in many urban wardrobes, few fashionistas realize the impact combat uniforms will have on future fashion.

The United States military has established research projects to develop new types of intelligent clothing for soldiers, which will enhance the protective and communicative properties of uniforms and combat gear. Projects initiated by DARPA (the Defense Advanced Research Projects Agency) and the United States Army are pioneering the development of new wearable technologies, and such military initiatives as Future Combat Systems, Future Force Warrior, Air Warrior and Mounted Soldier System are exploring the potential to create core garments that can be powered and controlled by wearable technology. Through collaborations with research teams based at such institutions as the University of California, Berkeley, and MIT, DARPA is also commissioning new types of headgear, body-mounted surveillance systems and wearable power sources.

Future combat uniforms will have sensory abilities and even appear to have an intelligence of their own. They will sense the impact of a bullet and send a signal to the soldier's command base, and will be able to administer medicine to wounded soldiers, detect poisonous gases and transmit reconnaissance intelligence. The uniforms will be engineered to change their colours and textures to match their surroundings, making printed camouflage patterns redundant (see Urban Camouflage, page 62). Such innovations pave the way for similar technologies to be incorporated into civilian clothing. Few fashion brands are able to make the large

investments required to develop such advanced technologies and make them wearable. Once these technologies have been fully developed by such organizations as DARPA, similar applications can be created for performance clothing and eventually adapted for everyday fashion.

One of the most visionary research and development projects in the United States military is the Future Force Warrior initiative. As the researchers engaged with the project explore the potential of such innovations as mechatronic exoskeletons (technological systems combining mechanical engineering and electronics, designed around the use and functions of the human body; see Superhuman Style, page 84), they are also pioneering the applications of nanotechnology for combat wear. Nanostructured systems (with structures sized between the molecular and the microscopic) are generally believed to be the gateway to the technology of the future. In terms of wearable technology, the unique behaviours of nanofibres give them sensing abilities and the ability to transmit information through their networks at rapid speeds.

Soldiers sent into combat zones typically wear bulky uniforms laden with heavy equipment. Attempts to create an exoskeleton that would weigh the same as, or less than, combat uniforms have so far failed, but when military clothing and equipment can be manufactured at the nanoscale they will be lighter and more durable. Nanotechnology will make it possible to incorporate a variety of functions into the fabric at a molecular scale, replacing bulkier embedded fibres. The garments that result will be a few millimetres thick and will fit close to the body, as a wetsuit does. Seamlessly integrated into the garment will be a network of fibre-based sensors

This X-ray of the suit worn by NASA astronaut Alan Shepard for his journey to the Moon in 1971 reveals the communications technology, life-support systems, radiation protection and temperature controls integrated in its stainless-steel fabric. Spacesuits continue to be a model for today's combat uniforms.

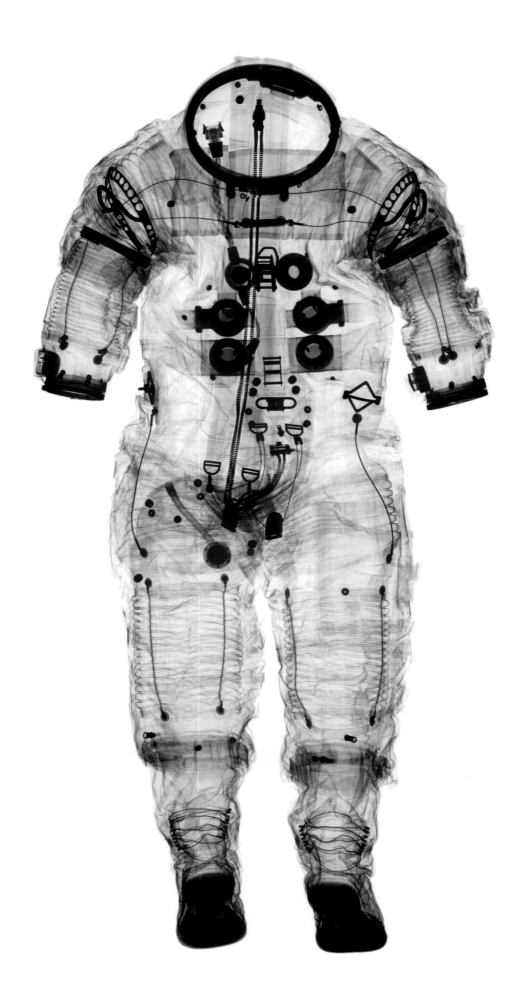

engineered to detect injury, which will trigger
responses by changing the properties of the material.
If bleeding occurs, for example, the fabric would
constrict around the wound to create a tourniquet.
Broken limbs would be reinforced immediately and
supported as the fabric around them became rigid.

The extent to which nanotechnology can make
significant differences to soldiers during combat is
being explored by a research team at MIT, which
includes scientists from the faculties of chemical,
mechanical, electrical and materials sciences, working
with US Army researchers and other scientific research
centres. The researchers believe that aspects of their
nanotechnology developments can benefit law
enforcement officers and security personnel, and
they make it available to other researchers. Their
'nanoscale origami' project, for example, engineers
nanoparticle composites with properties that can
create molecular chain mail. Researchers produced a
technique for folding thin films into individual three-
dimensional nanoscopic structures, linked at a
molecular level, which should have the same surface
tension, drape and fold as conventional metal mesh,

yet be much more resilient. This could create materials
that have the softness and flexibility of fashion
fabrics, but harden on impact to protect the wearer.

While state-of-the-art bulletproof vests are
being developed specifically for soldiers, researchers
also see the value of these vests to law-enforcement
officials, private security personnel and civilians.
Scientists at MIT's Hatsopoulos Microfluids Laboratory
are exploring the potential of magnetorheological
fluid (MR fluid, in which magnetic particles can
be aligned to increase resistance to penetration)
and magnetized textiles in bulletproof vests and
other protective garments. When fabric has been
saturated with MR fluid, the magnetic properties
remain in the fibres after the fabric has dried
and been made into clothing. Conductive wires
woven into the fabric are charged with electric
currents that wearers can control to create
different levels of rigidity, ranging from firm to
taut, and from rigid to rock-hard. When threatened
by attack, wearers can deploy the full magnetic
strength to maximize the garment's ability to
shield them.

SPORTSWEAR

At first glance, fashion and sportswear appear to be at opposite ends of the style spectrum. Fashion places emphasis on looks and trends, mostly targeted at female consumers, while sportswear delivers performance and functionality to a predominately male audience. While fashion garments are conceived of as tactile and smooth, sportswear's efficient surfaces are usually less inviting to the touch. Yet although high-performance training gear and style-centric fashions may seem irreconcilably diverse today, in the future there will be threads that bind them.

Few fashionistas realize that the sports industry is a market leader in developing fabric technology and high-performance designs; these strategies are currently being expanded for fashion in the form of multipurpose garments, integrated technology and high-performance textiles. Sportswear is encouraging the movement of materials and technologies across disciplines, taking high-performance fabrics into the collections of forward-thinking fashion designers. In common with clothing developed for military applications and space exploration, clothing created by the sports industry is often at the forefront of advanced textile developments. Sportswear designers engineer such innovations as compression technology and aerodynamic surfaces, and integrate phase-change materials (page 119), antibacterial fibres and deodorizing agents into clothing.

For many years, Nike has been a leader in developing sports apparel with a tailored fit and high-tech performance. Such sportswear ranges as Nike's Dri-FIT combine layers of hydrophobic (water-repellent) and hydrophilic (water-attracting) fabrics to move moisture away from the body. The underlayer is hydrophobic, neither absorbing nor

withholding the moisture; instead it functions as a pump or siphon, forcing the moisture to the hydrophilic layer on the garment's surface, which disperses the moisture by spreading it over a large area, where body heat and movement make it evaporate quickly. Similar moisture-control fabrics are being developed for fashion garments by such textile manufacturers as Teijin Fibers in Japan. Teijin's Sweat Sensor lining fabric is made with porous polymers that absorb perspiration and disperse it through a cross section of antibacterial fibres. The system is ideal for use in footwear, for example, but can also be integrated into fashion garments.

Nike has also developed sportswear surfaces that reduce drag, enabling athletes to run faster. The surface of its Swift Suit has less wind resistance than human skin, considerably improving the wearer's aerodynamic potential. The Nike Swift Suit worn by athletes at the 2008 Summer Olympics in Beijing was the most innovative of its kind. The suit was produced entirely from polyester yarns made from recycled plastic bottles and textile waste. The fabric and suit were crafted in a single expression using no-sew technology, making the suit virtually seamless, and mesh-like panels for ventilation were created by manipulating fibres as the garment was being made. By customizing the suit's fit on individual athletes, such technology further enables athletes to increase their clothing's aerodynamic potential.

In 2008 sports- and swimwear label Speedo launched the LZR Racer suit (pronounced 'laser'), which also featured at the Beijing Olympics. The technologized fabric was woven from lightweight, polyurethane-coated fibres, and was designed and engineered to perform in the manner of a shark's

The garments presented in Stella McCartney's Autumn/ Winter 2011–12 collection included close-to-the-body cuts that gave them an athletic feel. Contrasting panels and sleek silhouettes have more in common with performance sportswear than with mainstream fashion.

China's speed skater Wang Beixing won the 2009 World Sprint Speed Skating Championships for Women, held in Moscow. In competition, she dresses from head to toe in garments made from technical fabrics that are engineered to reduce drag.

skin, therefore reducing drag. The fabric was created in collaboration with NASA and the Australian Institute of Sport, and was given a cutting-edge appearance by motifs designed by Comme des Garçons. The LZR Racer also has a 'core stabilizer' that adds corset-like support to the fabric covering the abdominal area. Although the garment has visible seams, these are ultrasonically welded to reduce drag further.

Both Nike's Swift Suit and Speedo's LZR Racer have had an impact on other areas of apparel. All-in-one garments, seamless surfaces and polyurethane coatings are now common features of high-performance design, and custom-fit garments are regarded as an emerging trend. As fashion manufacturers begin adapting these innovations for a wider market, such innovations as 3D printing, which creates seamless garments, and body-scanners, which render custom fits, are gaining currency in mainstream fashion.

The Vortex 2 speed-skate suit launched in 2002 by Japanese sportswear label Descente was characterized by silicone ribs that improved the skater's stability, and by the use of compression to reduce drag. By using pressure to contract body tissue, the suit made the wearer's body more precisely contoured, and hence more aerodynamic.

Similar methods are used by fashion designers today. The emergence of 'shapewear', body-shaping garments designed to lift and sculpt fatty tissue, has showed the extent to which compression technology could create a more idealized shape. Compression undergarments are intended to give the wearer a slim and shapely appearance, mimicking the toned appearance of an athlete. Compression garments can have other benefits, too: when engineered to provide the

correct amount of surface pressure to specific parts of the body, they enhance blood circulation and channel more oxygen to active muscles. As a result, they can boost the wearer's stamina and strength in day-to-day activities as well as during exercise.

The pursuit of healthy bodies and a fit appearance has created a demand for garments that bridge the gap between sportswear and everyday clothing. For example, the NuMetrex line of athletic apparel uses 'smart fabric' technology that integrates textile electrodes into the garments' fabric to monitor the wearer's heart rate. The garments can be worn during exercise, removing the need for the heart-rate monitor that top athletes often wear during training to help them improve their timing and performance, and that some gym-goers use to monitor their metabolism and weight loss. Yet the garments are equally effective when worn as part of an ordinary outfit: during everyday activities, the sensors can help people to keep pace with their fitness goals, as indicators enable wearers to gauge if they are expending energy at a pace that helps them to burn body fat and improve their resting metabolism rate. Because the textile electrodes are knitted into the fabric, they stretch and move with the wearer, maintaining contact with the body and constantly sensing heart rate. A minute transmitter attached to the garment relays the heart rate to a compatible wearable device or exercise machine, giving the wearer a digital report.

Many types of performance sportswear have a protective function, keeping the wearer comfortable and dry in inclement weather and during extremes of temperature. Phase-change materials, for example, were developed for warming athletes on long-range winter-sports competitions without

FAR LEFT
The Superkini, produced by
O'Neill, a leading innovator
in swimwear design, is made
with Teijin Fibers' Nanofront
polyester. The material sticks
to the body when wet (see
page 117), preventing it from
gaping open or sliding out
of place.

LEFT AND BELOW
The NuMetrex Heart Sensing
Sports Bra and Heart Sensing
Racer Tank integrate electronic
sensing technology directly
into the fabric. A small
transmitter tucks into a
pocket to transmit data to
a heart-rate monitor or other
monitoring device.

OPPOSITE
Rick Owens's Spring/Summer
2011 menswear collection
included loose, comfortable
clothing in oversized cuts that
moved easily on the body. The
collection was infused with
energy and dynamism, carried
out in designs that had the
performance of sportswear.

causing them to overheat. The materials have
thermodynamic properties that enable them to
melt and solidify at certain temperatures. As
the materials change from solid to liquid, and vice
versa, they can both hold significant amounts of
energy and release stored energy. When phase-
change materials are incorporated into fashion
garments, they can create a comfort zone for the
wearer by maintaining a constant temperature
around the body.

The expertise of sportswear brands is
helping fashion designers to find solutions for
some of the challenges that ordinary clothing
cannot meet. The demand for custom-fit clothing
that can assist in fitness goals and offer personal
climate control is growing among mainstream
consumers. As these wishes come together in
single garments, the boundaries between high-
performance sportswear and high-tech clothing
promise to disappear completely.

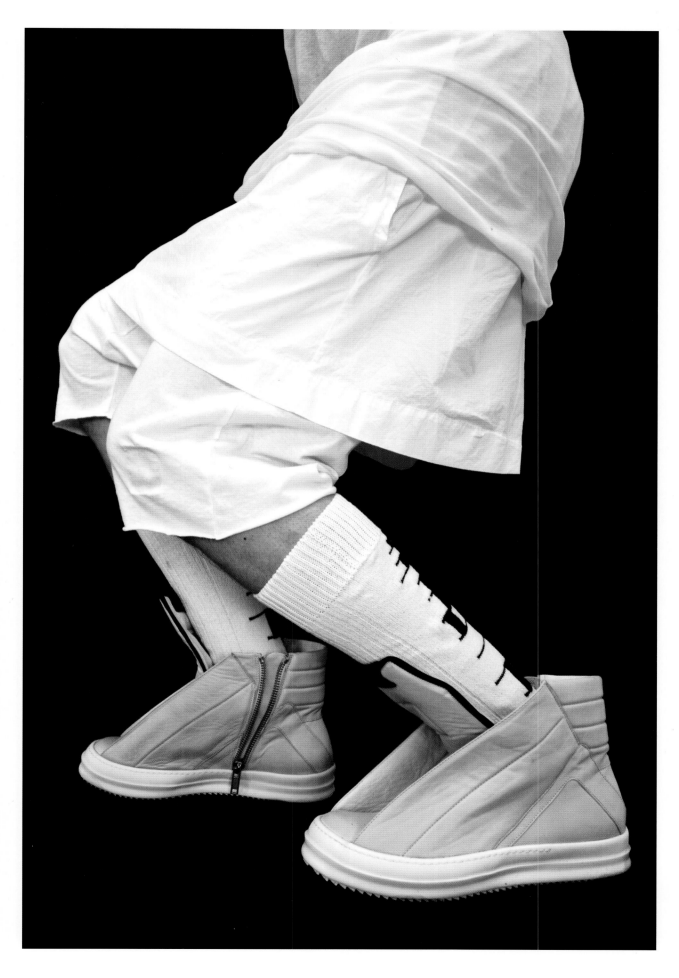

SUPERHUMAN STYLE

Stories of superheroes have dominated comic books for nearly a century, and have an established fan base in the film world. Their tales of strength, stealth and superhuman abilities inspire designers and technologists today, and the drive to replicate superhero powers in the form of wearable devices is likely to continue long into the future. Such characters as Superman, Captain America and Iron Man are committed to fighting for the public good, requiring clothing that protects them when in combat with their adversaries and provides them with the means of stealth and escape if defeated. The superhero's wardrobe, though fictional, is comprised of the ultimate high-performance clothing.

Most superheroes have enhanced senses. They might also have an innate ability to camouflage themselves, be able to fly through the air at great speed, or have the power to project energy bolts that wound, stun or destroy people and places. Their garments are form-fitting, shape-shifting and often enhanced with communications technology. A superhero's clothing is indestructible, offering armour-like protection or forming a visible exoskeleton around the body. Such attributes can be produced by technology, and when integrated into garments they enable fashion to re-create some superhuman abilities. Such designs as the No-Contact jacket (page 73) deploy an electric charge that mimics the energy surge superheroes can emit.

Ordinary humans can already soar through the sky at great speed, Superman-style, using wing suits, wearable devices constructed from performance fabrics. Atair Aerospace has designed a flexible wing suit known as the AeroSuit, which enables a skydiver to glide to a target far away from the drop point. The AeroSuit's arms and legs are fitted with inflated webbed panels that give the limbs wing-like properties. The panels dramatically improve the skydiver's aerodynamics, enabling a freefall drop to be transformed into a flight that covers considerable distances. Atair Aerospace's EXO-X2 wing suit is more rigidly structured than the AeroSuit, and is made for use with a turbine-powered engine so small and lightweight that it fits on the back like a backpack. As the engine is further developed to be more powerful and compact, it will enable the wing suit to lift off like a rocket, propelling the wearer into the air in the manner of a superhero taking flight.

Protective clothing has improved dramatically in recent years, and is now being constructed from new materials that make it fireproof and impact-resistant yet lightweight and supple. Such garments as the high-performance motorcycle racing suits created by Hyod (page 67) give the wearer unprecedented protection, mimicking the indestructibility of a superhero's uniform. Hyod's designs are typically comprised of some 300 different parts, made from materials chosen for their resilience, elasticity and ability to absorb impact and disperse it. Kevlar meshes and leather panels create a snug fit that moves easily with the body, while protective padding is made from D30, a soft impact-absorption material that has been molecularly engineered to rigidify when struck (see page 112).

Nanoscale technology can be used to create chain mail-like structures that can be integrated into fabric, giving garments the potential to repel bullets, thwart punches and resist knife slashes. Researchers at MIT have discovered that nanoparticles of such metals as iron can be manipulated by magnets, and can be used to create garments that stiffen when exposed to a magnetic field.

Dolce & Gabbana's Spring/Summer 2007 collection featured strong silhouettes and tough materials, bringing fortified fashion to the catwalk. The polished-metal piece shown here equips the wearer with a superhero-like shield that could deflect any blow.

The magnetic current changes the textile's properties dramatically, instantaneously transforming it from a soft-textured material to rigid matter. Depending on the level of magnetic polarity channelled through the fabric, the degree of rigidity ranges from firm to rock-hard. When the magnetic field is reduced, the garment immediately returns to its labile form. The garment is equipped within the fabric with the means to create a magnetic field, which the wearer can control. At the flip of a switch, the garment can rigidify to protect the wearer, even to the extent of becoming bulletproof. Although actual garments using this technology have not yet been commercially fabricated, the project has moved far beyond the theoretical stage.

Superheroes are expected to be super-strong, and the development of mechatronic systems designed to follow the shape and movements of the human body can give mere mortals unprecedented strength. In the future, motorized mechanical suits may even be a part of everyday life. Fitted with segments and joints that correspond to the body, they sit close to the skin and, thanks to inbuilt software, can be controlled by normal bodily reflexes. Sensors in the suit identify routine motions and areas of resistance, instructing the fabric lining the affected muscle groups to contract automatically. For example, when the wearer clasps an object, the fabric automatically constricts across the fingers and palm and tightens the grip considerably. As sensors identify a pulling motion, fabric contracts around the forearm, bicep and shoulder, boosting

LEFT
All-Star's baseball and softball batting gloves are produced with D30, which rigidifies when struck (see page 112), to make them more flexible while also protecting the wearer from the repeated impact of the hard ball on the bat – and occasionally the hand.

BELOW
These comfortable stretch shorts for men and women, produced by Icon, are fitted with removable pads at the hips to protect areas where some martial arts practitioners are likely to be kicked.

RIGHT
This compression top from Spyder is designed with an ergonomic fit. Its seamless construction eliminates points that could chafe the skin, the compression system offers comfortable support, and strategic vents cool the wearer by channelling air to areas where body heat builds up.

BELOW
Durable, lightweight and comfortable, and very efficient at absorbing impact, D3O is a popular choice for knee and elbow guards in motorcycle suits, which need to perform with the same flexibility as the human joint.

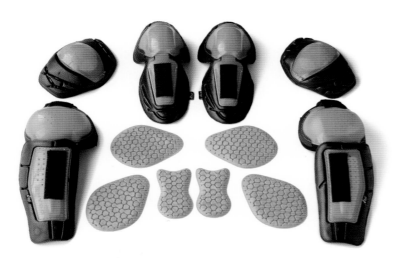

the wearer's strength. Such mechanical support systems have not yet been integrated into clothing, but garments using the technology could be worn by soldiers, construction workers and climbers, or anyone needing to boost strength.

As well as being strong, superheroes have heightened senses. So-called 'smart' garments that sense and react to stimuli around them would be able to broaden wearers' experience of their environment. Sensor networks could glean information from pressure actuators to gauge data about approaching objects. Biosensors (devices using biological molecules to detect the presence of chemicals) could identify others' gender, detect their emotional state and scan them for forensic evidence that would reveal where they had just been. Clothing that can 'see' and 'smell' on behalf of the wearer will have many practical applications. When worn by the blind, for example, the garment could provide warnings about approaching objects or locate specific items. For workers in the chemical industry, the garment could 'smell' leaching toxins and 'see' leaking gases, and alert the wearers before harm was caused.

Just as the creators of fictional superheroes gave them superhuman powers, future fashion designers will invent garments that endow their wearers with extraordinary abilities, yet the clothes will be worn by real people, in real situations. Future fashions will change dramatically as a result, and many of the limitations humans face today will become a thing of the past.

MARIA JANSSEN

London-based fashion designer Maria Janssen worked as a design director at Nike before joining global trend consultancy WGSN in 2007 as managing editor for youth, street and sport. Born in The Netherlands, Janssen studied fashion at London's Central Saint Martins College of Art and Design before embarking on a career in performance sportswear design, through which she gained an awareness of markets, materials and future directions. Today she is WGSN's creative director, leading a global team of researchers who identify emerging trends in sportswear and many other aspects of fashion. In her interview for this book, Janssen highlights how future fashion will be based on more than design trends alone, taking shape in response to consumer input, technological developments and new ways of gauging market shifts.

Are there any trends in street- and sportswear today that will be influential in the future?
We are seeing two interrelated trends that will have impact on youth culture for seasons to come. We call the first one 'Jpeg Gen'. This trend is about the emergence of the online generation, the first generation that has never known a world in which the internet did not exist. They have taken the language of the internet, one that is fast-reacting and multi-contextual, and made it their own. They live their lives in a series of screen grabs and are image circulators by nature. This has given rise to a trend that captures this generation's absurd wit, irony and the unexpected. It's about an aesthetic of speed over process, and crude computer craft combining jarring scale and motifs into unusual textures, bringing about an aesthetic revolution. Having grown up with the latest technology at their fingertips, this generation's youth view science and technology intuitively and through a different lens from previous generations. Nothing surprises them, and the impossible is possible.

Jpeg Gen is sparking a second trend, which will give rise to an aesthetic that celebrates the scientific and technical, creating a visual world that was once fantasy but is now becoming real.

Will fashion consumers have different expectations in the future?
Future consumer expectations will be high, and also demanding. The internet has created a consumer who is better informed and educated in fashion than before – think of the enduring trend for anything vintage that has developed from the huge amount of vintage info and product available online today. People expect a level of input into product development, and this is likely to replace our current understanding of 'customizable' product, in which the focus is on adapting and personalizing existing product as opposed to the consumer input into the design and development process that we will see in the future. Consumers will understand their collective power and expect to be listened to. Having grown used to technology, future consumers will demand a seamless connection between technology and their needs, their lifestyle.

Will performance fashion be trend-based?
Fashion will always be trend-based. There is always new talent with fresh ideas emerging that will drive fashion in new directions. The world changes day by day, and fashion will continue to reflect this.

How will fashion forecasting be done in the future?
In the past, forecasting was done by a few who created a seasonal (at times visionary) message that then trickled down into collections, then into the stores and ultimately to consumers. WGSN recognizes the opportunities provided by the internet to help to create forecasting as we know it now, making it more democratic (not just trickling down from the top) through constantly evolving analysis combined with expertise and intuition.

As multiple layers of trends develop at different rates, seasonal styles can overlap with one another and new global markets emerge. Forecasting will increasingly look at the complete 'lifespan' of a product, from long-term direction and close-to-season trends to the accurate prediction of short-term buying patterns (thanks to the analysis of online data). Parallel to this, we see an increase in a 'made-to-measure' approach. No longer is it enough to be 'on trend', and as everyone seeks to reduce risk it becomes increasingly important to select the right trends relevant to your 'brand' and market.

What is your vision for how WGSN's cohesive creative direction will unfold in future?
I'd like to see WGSN creative direction become an all-encompassing portfolio relevant across all the design and creative industries. It will be a holistic and user-friendly journey that uses the best creative minds to take clients from big-picture thinking through to execution, to market and beyond.

People belonging to the consumer group identified by trend consultancy WGSN as 'Jpeg Gen' absorb and filter information at a great rate. Maria Janssen says that these individuals make sense of the nonsensical by assigning data to the categories 'like' and 'dislike', editing life experiences as a curator would choose objects for an exhibition. This graphic represents that approach, showing that pastiche and montage may form a new visual language in the near future.

SARAH BRADDOCK CLARKE

Sarah Braddock Clarke is a British writer, curator and consultant who lectures at University College Falmouth in Cornwall, where she works on the fashion design and performance sportswear design BA (Hons) degrees. Co-author of *Techno Textiles* (1999), *Techno Textiles 2* (2005) and *SportsTech* (2002), Braddock Clarke is a leading expert in the field of fashion and performance sportswear. Her research focuses on emerging technologies and new materials, and explores the impact of digital media on textiles created for both fashion and sportswear. Often called upon to identify the materials and designs that are taking clothing into the future, she has looked to film and science fiction to predict what humans will be wearing in the decades to come. When interviewed for this book, Braddock Clarke described how innovation and tradition will work together in the future, pointing out how cutting-edge materials can be paired with natural fabrics, and how time-honoured tailoring techniques can underpin innovative technologies.

Where are new fashion and sportswear coming together today?

Fashion has given sportswear a chicer look, and sportswear is making mainstream clothing more comfortable. Comfort is as important in fashion as it is in sport; after all, you cannot be truly elegant if you don't feel at ease in what you are wearing.

How is performance sportswear influencing fashion today?

Many new materials and technologies coming into mainstream fashion today were originally developed for use in the area of high-performance sportswear. Body-conscious looks are being adopted from sportswear, and design elements are being introduced that were created for protective motorbike wear, surf wear, snowboard wear, skate wear, cycling wear, equestrian wear, tennis wear and so on. The looks that result link the wearer to a sporty lifestyle. Right from the start of the design process, manufacturers are considering how the garment can make the wearer look and feel better psychologically and physically. This is because such styles enable wearers to look as if they have the right balance of work and play, and possess a healthy body and an active mind. Rather than seeming like a workaholic, the wearer appears to be passionate about life and leisure.

Which performance sportswear labels are most innovative?

The big surf labels, such as Quiksilver, O'Neill, Oakley, Rip Curl, Animal and Billabong, invest in the latest materials and technologies, developing clothes that protect the wearer

from cold water and that are also extremely comfortable and look good. For example, O'Neill's Superkini [page 82] combines good looks with advantageous technology, exemplifying how fashion and sport can work well together. Advertised as 'the bikini that sticks with you', it is made from an ultrafine polyester nanofibre by Teijin Fibers called Nanofront, which, because it has a larger surface area than normal fibres, exerts a frictional force that enables it to grip the skin superbly. It feels and looks soft and silky, but is high-performance and will cope with the wearer diving off rocks and paddling through waves to haul herself up to stand on a board.

Another example is Oakley's Blade surfing board shorts, which enhance power, endurance and balance by using dual-construction technology for a two-layer garment. The underlayer is tight and stretchy, like cycling shorts, and is made of techno materials incorporating a high-performance compression liner. This holds the muscles in place and prevents muscle fatigue, so the wearer will recover well from physical exertion and get less 'muscle burn'. As the muscles are supported, the wearer will be less likely to pull a muscle or get cramp, and this layer also offers real comfort, with no rash-inducing rubbing. The outer layer looks like more traditional board shorts but is made from a superlight, non-absorbent hydrophobic material that will not become heavy in the water and dries very quickly.

In what ways will performance sportswear and fashion come together in the future?

I foresee the very body-conscious look pervading in future, with its figure-hugging and wrapping (sometimes with more than a nod

to fetish wear) in various degrees of stretch – elastostretch, ultra-stretch, super four-way stretch and engineered stretch. I also anticipate a look that relates the human form to the space around it, linking fashion with architecture in sculptural, anthropomorphic and ergonomic ways by using materials that possess a 'body' of their own. In addition, the use of digital technology to design and manufacture clothing on demand offers scope for individuals to be able to have clothing made to their own specifications.

Which of today's materials will continue to be used in future performance clothing?

Wool has many advantageous inherent properties, and I see it as a naturally high-performance material, one that will continue to be used for both cold-weather wear and, in lightweight form, warm-weather wear. Cotton's super-absorbency can impart great advantages, and everyone enjoys its look and feel – this will continue, I am sure. Likewise, such tough materials as denims and leathers will always have a role to play in both fashion and sportswear. The very latest treatments for denim render this hard-working material soft and yielding, while thin leathers provide second-skin protection.

I also see a place for non-textile materials, such as various woods, plastics, resins, carbon fibres and metals. These are being used in collections where they can provide strength, durability and longevity. Technology has allowed such rigid materials to become flexible and therefore able to be used in fashion and sportswear. Ultrasoft and ultralight materials are also being used to cushion and protect, as shown in the development of air-based materials, 'memory' foams, closed-cell foams and gels. These can absorb shock on impact and distribute it evenly, and they have had a profound influence on performance clothing. For example, aerogel [gel in which the liquid component has been replaced with a gas; first created in 1931] offers supremely lightweight thermal insulation.

To sum up, I see the future for performance clothing as being the application of flexible, yielding, absorbing materials from all branches of materials science – both textile and non-textile. It is an exciting area to be researching.

Surfwear and snowsports labels develop new materials and technologies to find ways to protect the wearer from cold and falls while making him or her look and feel good. In Rip Curl's 'dry in a flash' Flash Bomb wetsuit (shown bottom left and, inside-out, top right), water is rapidly funnelled out of the lining so that the suit dries quickly once it is removed, ensuring that surfers no longer have to put on a wet, cold wetsuit from the day before. The skiing and snowboarding thermal undershorts (top left) and vest (bottom right) produced by French label Pull-in are made of sweat-wicking Therma fabric and feature impact-absorbing panels of D3O (see page 112).

MAVER
MATER

**BIODYNAMIC
CONDUCTIVE
ELASTIC
PROTECTIVE
REACTIVE
REGENERATIVE**

**Interviews with
CHARLES SPENCE
MARIE O'MAHONY**

ICK
IALS

Advanced materials, both existing and under development, give garments a range of new capabilities, extending the functionality of clothes and widening their appeal

The worlds of fashion and materials science are merging. As soft material substrates and fibre technologies emerge, they spark potential for fresh innovations within fashion design. Electronic textiles, phase-change materials, bioengineered fibres and reactive coatings are opening new horizons, often aligning clothes more closely with technology than with traditional fashion. High-performance fibres, coupled with conductive materials, can transform garments into interactive devices that link wirelessly with other systems, assemblages of active materials that have the ability to communicate and interact, and can change colour, texture and form.

Advanced materials give garments a range of new capabilities, extending the functionality of clothes and widening their appeal. Materials that change shape when they detect body heat can automatically adjust clothing to the wearer's physique in order to ensure a perfect fit. Exciting colours and surface patterns can be created by fabrics interwoven with optical fibres or light-emitting diodes (LEDs), which can be programmed to reconfigure, pulsate and illuminate. Fabrics are manufactured with wear and tear in mind to reveal new colours, textures and motifs as they degrade through routine use. Textiles engineered by scientists and microbiologists could react more in the manner of living tissue than of fashion fabric, even lining the body with a living second skin of bacteria.

These crossover materials mark a specific moment in fashion, in which garments are beginning to be characterized by hybrid forms, and are in themselves emerging as complex, multi-faceted hybrids. Their ability to mimic natural processes is changing the way the human body is experienced, while their capacity to interact with urban technologies is influencing the way the technological systems are built. For such wireless interaction to work smoothly, user-friendly parameters are being factored into the design of wearable technology, and hence into the garments themselves. This is giving wearers a central role in the development of materials, and fashion fabrics are beginning to be created with a wider spectrum of consumer needs in mind.

OPPOSITE
Diana Eng's Fairytale Fashion collection of 2010 consisted of clothing equipped with wearable technologies, phase-change materials and reactive coatings. Such garments as the Twinkle dress and cardigan, shown here, change shape and colour.

PAGES 96–97
Volume can be created in garments through the use of shape-changing materials, but Eng's folding textile achieves the same effect thanks to a low-tech method: Miura-ori. Based on the principles of origami and developed by Japanese astrophysicist Koryo Miura, Miura-ori enables the fabric to deploy and fold again quickly and easily. The photographs show Eng's red deployable hoodie and pale blue puff-sleeve jacket.

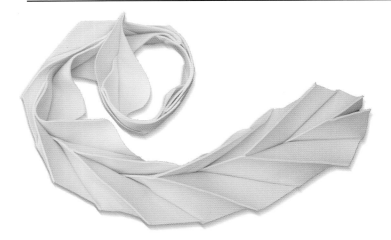

Although high-tech materials are taking fashion into the future, they still have to perform in the manner of traditional fabrics. Touch-sensitive textiles, for example, which are used as control panels for mobile phones and other wireless devices, are soft enough to be integrated into garments, but cannot yet withstand the rigours of a conventional washing machine. To meet the consumer norm of washing garments in water at home, the next generation of touch-sensitive textiles is being made tough enough to withstand the hot cycle. Most wearable microelectronic components are unlikely to become washable in the near future, inciting technologists to develop 'no-wash' fabrics that need never be immersed in water. Coated with substances that enable dirt, dust and perspiration simply to roll off, the fabrics provide an ideal substrate for technologies that cannot come into contact with water.

Future fashion materials will have to be broader in scope and more expansive in reach in order to cater for a greater range of applications than they currently do. Many leading manufacturers already include in their basic lines a variety of technical textiles, which are tailored for many types of clothing genres. Eco-friendly fabrics, such as those described in the 'Biodynamic' section (page 102), are a must for manufacturers producing sustainable fashion. These fabrics are derived largely from untraditional fibres, or produced using new processes that consume less water and energy than conventional methods. Some of the textiles featured in the 'Conductive' section (page 106) are made for aerospace and computer hardware applications,

and have the potential to be produced in bulk as demand for wearable technology increases.

The market for strong, stretchable and lightweight textiles gets bigger each season. Among the materials described in the 'Elastic' section (page 110) are impact-absorbing substrates that function as shock absorbers, and shape-memory materials that morph and deform, yet revert to their original shape. As also illustrated in the 'Reactive' section (page 118), future fashion materials will be more fluid than fixed, responding, changing and adapting to sets of preprogrammed parameters.

Consumers' desire for greater personal security is driving designers to create performance garments that make the wearer feel safe. The 'Protective' section (page 114) describes some of the materials that can shield the body, thwart attackers and guarantee a product's authenticity. With the need to protect comes the drive to prevent setbacks, making wellness and vitality areas of importance for textile developers. Fabrics featured in the 'Regenerative' section (page 122) show that future garments will be able to diagnose physical problems and medicate wearers, as well as boost their vitality by delivering vitamins and stimulants through the skin.

The materials featured in this chapter reveal that textile innovation is rapidly transforming our world. High-tech materials, nature's processes and scientific research are creating groundbreaking fabrics. Fashion may soon become characterized by technological innovations and striking silhouettes, but its future will be moulded by the materials from which it is made.

LEFT
Diana Eng's Miura-ori pleated scarf is a biomimetic design that mimics the folding contours of the hornbeam leaf, which help the leaves to open as they grow in spring. The voluminous scarf's space-saving design means that it folds easily for compact storage.

OPPOSITE
Sabine Seymour is known for her pioneering use of technology and her innovative approach to materials. For her Zebra-print T-shirt, she lists sunlight among the materials used to make it, as solar energy is required to make the zebra's head appear.

Diana Eng's research into integrating deployable structures within fashion is pioneering. These images show the dramatic transformation that occurs in her Inflatable Dress, made from silk chiffon draped over inflatable plastic forms, when the inflatables are deployed.

BIODYNAMIC

Many of the new developments in materials science are driven by consumer concerns about sustainability and the environment. Some scientists are drawn to emulating the living systems of animals and plants, developing biodynamic textiles based on processes that occur in the natural world. As a result, new horizons for fashion and textile design are emerging. Fabrics formed from seaweed cellulose, vegetable fibre and self-binding filaments are becoming popular alternatives to cotton and linen cloth and synthetic textiles. Discarding the image of hemp-heavy hemlines and rough-and-ready textures, the new sustainable textiles are as soft to the touch as they are gentle to the planet.

Advances in biopolymer science are making it possible to replace synthetic textiles with organic fabrics derived from plant-based polymers. Polymer fibres, which are made from bonded molecules or other units, are generally lighter, thinner, softer, less expensive to produce and more colour-fast than other types of fibre, and clear polymers can create fibres with translucent properties. Polymer foams are firm and dense, yet mouldable and easy to print on, making them ideal for fashion applications. The materials featured in this section are derived from surprising processes, revealing the extent to which nature and science can come together in fabric form.

OPPOSITE
Malaysian sustainable fashion label Ultra uses surprising materials for fashion. This dress is crafted from fish-skin leather. The discarded skins of farmed fish can be tanned in the same way as most animal leathers, providing a durable alternative to bovine sources.

AirDye
Traditional methods of dyeing garments use very large volumes of water as well as substantial amounts of energy. Researchers at Colorep, a sustainable-technology company based in California, set out to develop a means of dyeing and printing fabric without using water or liquid dyes. The AirDye process transfers proprietary dyes from paper on to fabric using heat only, and the method is entirely waste-free. No pollutants are released, the paper is recycled, and used dyes and toners are also recycled into additives that colour asphalt and tar. AirDye is available in a kaleidoscope of colours, and can be engineered to match traditional dyes and to colour a wide range of fabrics. Pictured above are two pieces from the Spring/Summer 2010 collection by American label Costello Tagliapietra (Jeffrey Costello and Robert Tagliapietra), which premiered AirDye.

Biophyl

Most polyesters are made with petrochemicals, such as petroleum-based ethylene glycol. Biophyl fibres and yarns, produced by European polyester manufacturer Advansa, are made with polytrimethyl terephthalate (PTT), a new polymer developed to make polyester in which glycol is replaced with Bio-PDO, an organic compound made by DuPont Tate & Lyle from corn sucrose. In comparison to most fossil-based fabrics, the production of Biophyl requires much less energy: 30 per cent less overall, resulting in a 60 per cent reduction of greenhouse gas emissions, according to Advansa. Biophyl can be dyed at lower temperatures than traditional polyester, thus further saving energy and reducing costs.

Cocona

By incorporating organic materials into polymers, the American company Cocona has developed a performance fibre harvested from nature. The fibre is bound with activated carbon (carbon that has been processed to make it extremely porous) made from coconut shells, which neutralizes odour and wicks away perspiration. Cocona fibres and yarns can be used to make woven cloth and knitwear, and can also be used in non-woven fabrics. Cocona promotes evaporation of moisture, cooling the wearer, and provides protection against ultraviolet light from the sun, making it an excellent choice for warm-weather locations. Cocona's manufacturer claims that the product, which is hardwearing, supple and soft to the touch, may one day replace denim completely.

Eco Circle PlantFiber

The new polyester textile produced by Japanese manufacturer Teijin Fibers will soon make oil-based fabrics a thing of the past. Derived from plant-based polyethylene terephthalate (PET), Eco Circle PlantFiber is becoming Teijin Fibers' most popular bio-fabric for fashion applications. Biofuels derived from sugar cane and other biomass (organic matter) are used in the fabric's production, further reducing the amount of fossil resources used in its manufacture. The fabric can be recycled using Teijin Fibers' Eco Circle polyester recycling system, which chemically decomposes the fabric at a molecular level before recycling it as dimethyl terephthalate (DMT; used in the production of polyesters).

SeaCell

Seaweed cellulose can be dissolved and combined with cellulose from other plant material to create fibres that medicate the skin (seaweed cellulose contains minerals and other active substances that have an anti-inflammatory effect and are also effective in the treatment of the chronic skin condition prurigo). SeaCell, from German company smartfiber, is made using the same process as the viscose (wood-pulp-based) Lyocell (also known as Tencel), resulting in fibres that have high strength under both wet and dry conditions; this makes them ideal for use in socks, for example, such as those made by Swiss company Rohner (above). The fibres can be coloured by conventional dyes, and their performance is similar to that of Lyocell and other viscose fibres.

Sorona

Polymers derived from plants rather than fossil fuels are a popular choice for textile manufacturers. The Sorona plant-based polymers developed by DuPont's biotech division are extruded into a strong, soft and highly stain-resistant fibre that can be blended easily with other fibres, and woven or knitted into high-quality fabric. Sorona can also be used to make films and coatings that can be applied directly to fabrics.

Zelfo

Paris-based materials research laboratory Zelfo Technology has developed a method of recycling cellulose fibres into a self-binding material that is an economical, adaptable and sustainable alternative to plastics and a range of other materials. The Zelfo material was developed specifically to provide an alternative to non-renewable materials. Zelfo Technology is collaborating with Toulouse-based laboratory Agromat to develop fibres for fashion applications, including fabric, padding and footwear.

CONDUCTIVE

Electronic textiles can enable clothing to function as computing devices, transmitting data via conductors, switches and sensors. Transistors and antennae can be created in fibre form and woven into garments so that they can communicate with remote systems. Threads coated with such metals as silver and nickel make excellent conductors, and ductile fibres (able to be deformed without losing toughness) made from such materials as carbon, polymers and finely drawn copper sit snugly on the body. Silicon chips and sensors can be downscaled to fibre-size and interwoven with plastic-threaded chip carriers and minute circuit boards. The wearable hardware that these create can sustain a range of software applications, and, as is the case with most computer devices, they can easily adapt to changes in the computational and sensing requirements of an application.

Wearable technology can evolve only at the same rate as the conductive materials that sustain it. Manufacturers active in this field are developing soft computer parts that can be worn comfortably on the body, engineering them to have the same strength and elasticity as most fashion fibres. Conductive textiles should be washable, flexible and lightweight, follow current style trends and enhance the wearer's physique. Although wearable technology is still an emerging genre within fashion, the conductive hardware that facilitates it is evolving at a rapid pace. As well as making conductive threads, manufacturers are producing textiles with coatings and films created with conductive polymers. The products that follow are making technology wearable today, and signal new directions for the haberdashery of the future.

PAGE 109
Electroluminescent wires are emerging as a favourite material of many designers. Diana Eng's luminescent EL Wire coat is crafted from layers of fabric fitted with sensors that detect motion, and the garment is trimmed with electroluminescent wires that light up in response to the wearer's movements.

AmberStrand

The lightweight conductive fibre AmberStrand is widely used in aerospace applications, and is often used in computing and wearable technology. AmberStrand is derived from the synthetic polymer fibre Zylon; Zylon fibres are coated with conductive metals, such as silver and nickel, then bundled together to form yarn. AmberStrand is emerging as an alternative to conductive threads made with beryllium copper alloy, which is toxic.

EeonTex

The EeonTex range of fabrics, yarns and foams made by Eeonyx, an American company specializing in conductive materials, has conductive nanoscale coating. The degree of conductivity is determined by the thickness of the coating, making the fabric's electrical capabilities fully customizable, and coatings of different thicknesses can be used to create surface patterns. EeonTex is suited to a large variety of applications, ranging from radar-avoidance suits and pressure-sensing fabric to touch-sensitive gloves and garments that take on different colours in response to changes in temperature.

Electroluminescent wires

Light-emitting surfaces give garments the potential to shine. Electroluminescent wires can illuminate an entire surface area or create patterns and colourways that light up at the flick of a switch, and they are low-voltage, making it possible to power a 30-metre-long (nearly 100 ft) length of wire with just a single one-amp fuse. A transformer is needed to adjust the intensity of the light and vary the shades of colour, which are determined by optic wavelengths rather than colour particles. Low frequencies create soft colour shades or pastel hues, while high frequencies deepen the colours and give them more intensity.

Diana Eng's luminescent EL Wire dress (above), crafted from silk chiffon embellished with electroluminescent wire, translates the wearer's movements into spectacular light effects thanks to an accelerometer and circuit boards housed in a 3D-printed neckpiece.

Inherently conductive polymers (ICPs)

Researchers are integrating textiles and technology at molecular level in order to create stronger bonds between conductive polymers and the electronic circuitry integrated into the fabric. A patented technique developed collaboratively by scientists at Australia's Commonwealth Scientific and Industrial Research Organisation (CSIRO) and University of Wollongong binds inherently conductive polymers (ICPs, also known as intrinsically conductive polymers) indissolubly to the fabric's fibres, dramatically heightening the electroconductive properties of the textiles. The electronic conduction is so stable that the garment can be cleaned in a washing machine without any loss of conductivity. CSIRO's knee sleeve (above) gauges strain to help in reducing injuries, and the data it records on athletes' knee flexion angle can be used to help to enhance their performance.

Masa

Japanese technology developer Suzutora was the first to develop a method of applying nanoscale metal coatings to fabric, patented under the name Masa. The fibres can be made into a range of conductive textile substrates, including knitwear, woven fabrics and nonwoven membranes. Unlike the stiff metal-coated fibres created by plating or vapour-deposition methods, Masa fibres are as soft to the touch as they were in their untreated form. Masa is currently being engineered to withstand cleaning in conventional washing machines.

Optical fibres

While metal strands, such as electroluminescent wires (page 107), are an effective means of transmitting normal data, light and power through a textile substrate, optical fibres allow transmission at higher bandwidths. Made from such materials as silica, optical fibres are not liable to electromagnetic interference. Flexible and strong, they are compatible with most textile substrates, while their capacity to illuminate gives them the potential to create eye-catching embellishments on the surface. Optical fibres can also be used as sensors to gauge strain, temperature and pressure around the wearer.

Ultra-flexible cabling

Danish research laboratory Ohmatex has developed a conductive textile ribbon that can be sewn into garments to interconnect circuit boards, sensors and power sources. The advanced version, known as ultra-flexible cabling, is strong and supple enough to connect vibrating mechanical parts or components that are constantly in motion. This makes it useful in applications that require cabling that can be twisted, bent and stretched.

ELASTIC

Steel, cement and other rigid building materials are currently being engineered to be as flexible as they are strong. Among fashion materials the reverse is true: supple fibres are being enhanced with substances that increase their strength, yet enable them to retain their softness and tactility. Today strength alone is not enough to make any material competitive, and, in the future, tensile properties are likely to make or break a fibre's appeal. As in the case of building materials, new fashion fabrics are hard-wearing, able to repel water and dirt, and easy to care for, while being engineered to be more elastic.

As fashion fabrics move forward, they are evolving into substrates that work in combination with other materials. The synergy between them results in multilayer fabrics, fibrous composites and other hybrid forms that utilize the best properties of each. The combination of elasticity and strength can be found in a wide range of sources, and when created from natural substances, fibres can be both sustainable and strong. Several of those engineered by scientists and technologists can morph into new shapes and return to their original form again. Many are combined with conductive materials and advanced polymers, signalling the possibilities for creating a fabric so elastic it stretches the imagination to its limits.

OPPOSITE
When it comes to elasticity and strength, spider silk outperforms most other fibres. This researcher in Lyon, France, is harvesting silk from spiders' abdomens by means of revolving bobbins. Each spider can produce about 180 metres (590 ft) of silk an hour.

Aracon

Strong enough that it is considered to be an alternative to metal mesh, Aracon is constructed from a Kevlar base fibre that is coated with a metal compound often made from 100 per cent nickel or nickel/silver combinations. Developed by DuPont, the lightweight, highly flexible textile is strong enough to stop bullets yet elastic enough to move with the body. Aracon, in common with many other metal textiles, is electrically conductive and anti-static, and is able to provide barriers against both electromagnetic interference and radio-frequency interference.

Auxetic fabrics

While most materials get thinner when stretched and fatter when compressed, auxetic materials (from the Greek word *auxesis*, 'increase') do just the opposite: they get fatter when stretched, and thinner when compressed. These materials have a surprising reaction to impact and strain. Whereas most materials will stretch at the point of impact, becoming attenuated, auxetic materials compress at the point of impact, becoming denser. Few other materials demonstrate elasticity to this degree, making auxetic fabrics a material of choice for designers pioneering performance solutions.

D3O

This impact-resistant material is engineered with an elastic structure comparable to the movement of wet sand. When wet sand flows, the grains move smoothly, but when the sand is compressed, the grains lock together. D3O works in a similar way, locking fibres together upon impact and therefore absorbing and distributing the resulting energy, which protects the wearer; pictured above is the Stryker D3O-incorporating motorcyclist's knee pad by American firm Icon. D3O reveals new potential for elastic materials to interact with the body and its surroundings.

Lycra T400

A staple in stretch apparel, Lycra (the trade name for a brand of spandex, or elastane, made by the Invista multinational) has long been known for its exceptional elasticity. The Lycra T400 fibre, made from multi-component yarns, is one of the most resilient in the Lycra range. Unlike its predecessors, its elasticity is not compromised by bleaching, finishes, whisker washing (creating pale 'whisker' marks at crease points on trousers) or sandblasting. The fibre combines perfectly with denim to create stretch jeans that don't lose their elasticity, and it is chlorine-resistant, enabling it to withstand washing better than other types of stretch denim.

Shape-memory materials

Shape-memory materials, such as nitinol (a metal alloy of nickel and titanium), have the ability to change shape in response to a reduction in temperature and then revert to their original form when heated above their transformation temperature. In theory, it would be possible to produce a sleeveless summer dress that would expand when the temperature drops, lowering its hemline and growing around the wearer's arms.

Spider silk

Few would suspect that the proteins synthesized by spiders could produce filaments that are even stronger than carbon fibres, or that spider webs can have a tensile strength five times greater than that of high-grade steel. Spider silk is also amazingly elastic, being able to stretch up to 40 per cent of its length without breaking. When spun using the techniques employed to produce industrial thread (see page 111), spider silk can be made into yarns that stretch to a remarkable degree and as a result are virtually indestructible. Spider silk is considered to be a sustainable resource, since spiders consume renewable materials and synthesize them into fibres without producing harmful emissions.

Ultra-high-molecular-weight polyethylene

Ultra-high-molecular-weight polyethylene (UHMWPE) is formed into resilient fibres, such as Spectra and Dyneema, that have both strength and elasticity, and are able to be stretched and expanded exponentially to degrees that would snap most other fibres. These properties make them ideal for performance applications. As lightweight as they are stretchy and strong, UHMWPE fibres form the basis of most garments and equipment made for such extreme sports as climbing and paragliding.

PROTECTIVE

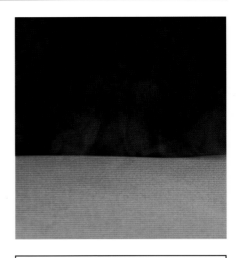

Concerns about personal security and safety are generating a demand for protective clothing, and urban dwellers want these garments to be as tailored and chic as the rest of their wardrobe. Materials developed for military combat uniforms and tactical wear are gradually filtering into fashion collections, bringing weatherproof coatings, abrasion-resistant textures and crash cushioning into day-to-day use. For example, the growing number of urbanites opting for two-wheeled transport is creating a bigger market for performance garments that are highly protective yet blend in with everyday clothing. This aspect of fashion promises to be a growth area in the future, and clothing that shields against radiation, pollution and other kinds of airborne toxins will soon find a market.

The need for protection is not limited to personal safety; fashion houses and other commercial entities need to safeguard against having their designs reproduced or their labels misrepresented. Fashion fabrics can now integrate a range of data-storing devices in order to identify and authenticate the manufacturer and the production methods. Counterfeit clothing and accessory 'fakes' will be easier for the consumer to spot, protecting the manufacturer's interests and discouraging copies. With future fashion expected to protect the manufacturer as well as the consumer, garments will provide security on many different levels.

c_change

Described by its developer, the Swiss textile company Schoeller, as a 'bionic climatic membrane', c_change is a wind- and waterproof membrane that reacts to changing temperatures. The fabric's structure opens as body heat rises, enabling excess heat and perspiration to escape; in cold weather, or when the wearer is inactive, body temperature is lower, so the fabric remains closed and retains heat directly on the body. As a result, c_change maintains an optimal body temperature and helps to keep the wearer dry.

Deflexion

Until recently, designers using performance fabrics had to choose between rigid, armour-like materials and soft yet sturdy and heavyweight materials. Deflexion, developed by the Dow Corning multinational, has emerged as a material that provides the benefits of both, but with fewer drawbacks. Lightweight and soft, Deflexion is a silicone-based impact-protection material that offers the reinforcement of armour with the comfort of a fashion fabric, and is flexible enough to be adapted for use in high-performance protective apparel for many different types of application.

DNAtex

Counterfeit fashion results in significant losses for manufacturers and retailers. For years fashion labels have been looking for an effective means of protecting themselves against illegal copying and fraudulent use of their labels. Schoeller proposed a solution when it introduced its DNAtex system, which marks fabrics with a range of invisible signifiers that makes each one unique. These signifiers can be read via a handheld electronic sensor, providing an efficient means of identifying and authenticating fabric.

Microtaggants

Other companies developing systems that help to prevent counterfeiting and fraud, such as Minnesota-based Microtrace, use 'taggant' technologies, in which minute quantities of reactive chemicals are incorporated into the production line in order to make it possible to trace every stage of the product's manufacture. Microtaggants can be produced in several forms, including powder, ink and compound plastic resins (above) that range in size from 20 microns (a micron being 1/1000 of a millimetre) to 1200 microns. They can be marked on any surface, making it possible to tag trim, gemstones or any other embellishments attached to a garment. Each reactive chemical has a specific wavelength, so that various parts of the garment can be differentiated.

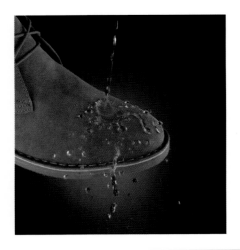

OPPOSITE
O'Neill's Superkini is made
from Teijin Fibers' ultrafine
Nanofront polyester, which
produces non-slip fabrics that
stick to the skin. The bikini
can withstand the force of
powerful waves without
slipping out of place.

P2i

The nanocoatings technology company P2i, based in Britain, has emerged in recent years as a world leader in liquid-repellent nanocoating processes, a technology that protects fabric and prevents it from being damaged by water, chemicals and dirt. P2i developed a process that significantly enhances a material's ability to repel liquid, causing any fluid that comes into contact with the material to form beads and simply roll off. As well as protecting the fabric and making the garment last longer, the technology also safeguards the wearer against contact with harmful substances.

Polymet

Polymet is a high-tech metal-plated fabric manufactured in both woven and non-woven versions, that was developed for aerospace applications. The fabric is tear-resistant, shields against high temperatures and protects against chemical contamination. The polymers forming the textile create a three-dimensional microporous structure that enables the material to be galvanized (coated with a protective layer). Polymet can be fabricated as a dense composite material or a thin membrane.

Vectran

Vectran, created by the Dallas-based Celanese Corporation, is emerging as a popular alternative to metal textiles and metal mesh. The fibre is made through a process of melt extrusion using liquid crystal polymer (LCP) pellets. The fabric's toughness, flexibility and resistance to abrasion and slashing endow it with properties far superior to those of a suit of armour. Although Vectran surpasses the strength of most other textiles, the attributes that make it so appealing also limit its usage: it defies conventional cutting and sewing operations, as normal cutting blades are dulled instantly because of the hardness and durability of the LCP used to produce the fibres. The fabric can be cut by using a heat process that warms the cutting tool's blade to a temperature slightly above the fibre's zero-strength temperature.

REACTIVE

Reactive surfaces give fabrics an extra dimension, boosting their potential to interact with humans and other objects. Garments equipped with touch-sensitive pads and haptic interfaces (such as gloves or control handles that simulate the feeling of touch) have added appeal, entreating wearers to engage with the fabric in ways that trigger changes in the material's surface. Surface sensors can respond to sunlight, wind, humidity and barometric pressure by changing colour or emitting light. Photoreactive coatings, thermosensitive dyes and light-reactive pigments enable patterns and motifs to change colour and return to their original design, creating new potential for future colourways. Microelectronic circuitry integrated within clothing will enable the surfaces of garments to change texture, while temperature-reactive materials will allow clothes to alter their shapes dramatically.

Future garments will react in other ways, too. Clothing made with contaminant-aware fabrics will alert wearers to potential dangers, protecting them behind a responsive shield. Substances that sense changes on the skin's surface will trigger the fabric to wick away moisture, or repel dirt. As clothing is given the potential to respond to the wearer and the environment, garments will be able to renew themselves.

Contaminant-aware fabric

Fabric printed with substances that react to airborne toxins or harmful bacteria would detect the presence of these dangers and alert the wearer. Current research in contaminant-aware fabrics explores the potential to encapsulate within the fibres minute electronic chips containing live nerve cells capable of detecting a range of chemical, radioactive and biological contaminants, which would trigger fabric woven with optic fibres, LEDs or light-emitting molecules to convey a simple warning to the wearer. The warning would not have to be high-tech; the garment could simply begin to discolour. Fabrics could also be endowed with self-decontaminating properties; for example, antibodies incorporated in the fibres could destroy certain contaminants on contact.

Phase-change materials

Phase-change materials (PCMs) contain innumerable microcapsules that react to temperature fluctuation by changing from solid to liquid and vice versa. The substances in the microcapsules have been set to a particular temperature range. If the wearer's body temperature or the outside temperature rises, the excess warmth is stored; when the temperature drops, the microcapsules change form and the stored warmth is released. PCM fabrics developed by such companies as Schoeller (pictured above) and the American firm Outlast keep the body warm even at relatively low temperatures over a long period, and, conversely, keep it cool in warm conditions and prevent it from overheating during exercise.

Quantum tunnelling composites

The assemblage of metals and non-conducting elastomeric binders (having elastic properties) known as quantum tunnelling composites (QTCs) reacts to contact by becoming conductive. Without pressure being applied, the conductive elements are not close enough to one another to conduct electricity; when the material is compressed, it forms a tunnelling process that facilitates the conduction of electricity on the surface of the material. When integrated into clothing (such as the No-Contact jacket shown above; see page 73), QTCs can be used to create a protective garment that emits an electric charge when gripped by an attacker; the shock stuns the attacker, giving the wearer a chance to get away.

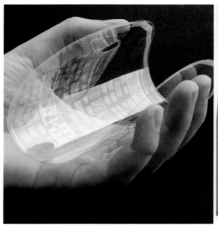 

Sensory textiles

Sensory textiles integrate into the structure of the fabric sensors capable of discerning changes in temperature, levels of ambient light, pressure and the wearer's gait, and of triggering responses. Garments made with such fabrics could detect darkness and react by emitting light, or, on an elderly person, could detect a fall and alert carers. Combined with microcapsule technology, sensory textiles could react to sunlight by releasing sunscreen to shield the wearer.

Thermochromic materials

Substances that can sense shifts in temperature and change colour accordingly are a popular source of innovation in fashion. 'Invisible' motifs printed with thermosensitive dyes become visible when exposed to warmth, or, alternatively, to cold, as in the scarf by American designer Diana Eng pictured above and opposite. Thermochromic pigments can be combined with such materials as rubber, plastic and foam, then applied to the garment as a coating. When combined with liquid crystal technology, thermochromic dyes enable a textile substrate to sense the energy released by the body and transform the appearance of the surface.

X-Bionic

The Swiss research and development laboratory X-Technology created the Xitanic sports fabric inspired by the desert fox's cooling coat of shiny fur, which deflects heat, and its large ears, which act as ventilators to release body heat. The company used these concepts in its X-Bionic partial compression material, which channels perspiration around the wearer's body to assist evaporation, creating a cooling effect.

REGENERATIVE

The drive towards wellness and vitality is influencing many consumer markets, and its impact on fashion is gaining momentum by the day. In the near future, fashionistas are likely to rate feeling healthy and looking young as highly as appearing stylish. Fashion brands are beginning to acknowledge the importance of health and well-being, as is reflected in designs that make wearers look fit and feel refreshed, and boost their sense of vitality. As a result, an exciting new area is emerging that links sportswear and protective clothing with medical science and gerontology.

One of the most revolutionary developments is taking place in health-care fabrics: textiles have been developed to deliver vitamins and medicine through the wearer's skin. Clothing with interwoven sensors can monitor the wearer's health, relaying real-time information to medical staff who may be able to make a diagnosis without even examining the patient. Robotic technology can be used to produce performance-boosting garments that provide additional sources of strength to support the wearer's movements. Such technologies will enable patients to function better in everyday life, and maximize the sense of vitality experienced by those aspiring to feel even better.

PAGE 124
Hard blows can bruise the skin, creating a visual record of the impact. A sensor-studded garment such as this one, designed by Adam Whiton and Yoda Patta, researchers at the Massachusetts Institute of Technology, can record assaults in the same way and transfer the data to a computer, providing a victim of domestic violence, for example, with a means of recording escalating abuse.

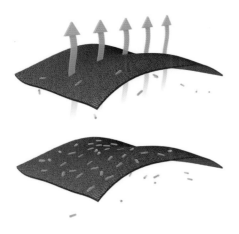

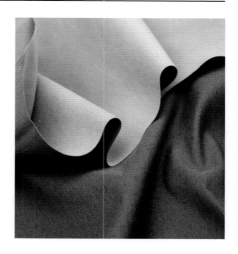

Active>silver

Silver salts repel bacteria, funguses and mites, can come into contact with skin without disturbing its flora, and discourage the growth of organisms that create odours and cause discoloration. Finishes derived from silver salts can be applied to almost any textile and used in combination with other finishes and coatings. When applied to clothing, the coatings create garments that remain hygienic and fresh for longer, effectively regenerating themselves. Schoeller's Active>silver finish permanently bonds the silver salts to the surface of the fabric, creating a long-lasting regenerative surface that withstands machine washing.

Electroactive polymer artificial muscle

The characteristics of human muscle have been reproduced in a textile membrane known as electroactive polymer artificial muscle (EPAM). The material is equipped with actuators connected to small, mobile robots and micromachine applications that imitate the way natural muscle works. In wearable form, EPAM encourages the wearer to reach optimal performance levels, preventing muscle strain. EPAM is considered to be a biomimetic device, as the robotic systems within are programmed to mimic the dexterity and mobility of humans.

Energear

The human body emits waves of heat, quantified scientifically as far infrared rays (FIR), which radiate away from the body. Schoeller's performance-enhancement Energear fabric reflects FIR back to the wearer, boosting blood circulation and increasing oxygen levels in the blood. This has a regenerative effect, as it enhances physical performance, improves concentration capacity and prevents premature fatigue. Energear fabric was designed for athletes but has since proven its worth in mainstream sportswear and fashion garments.

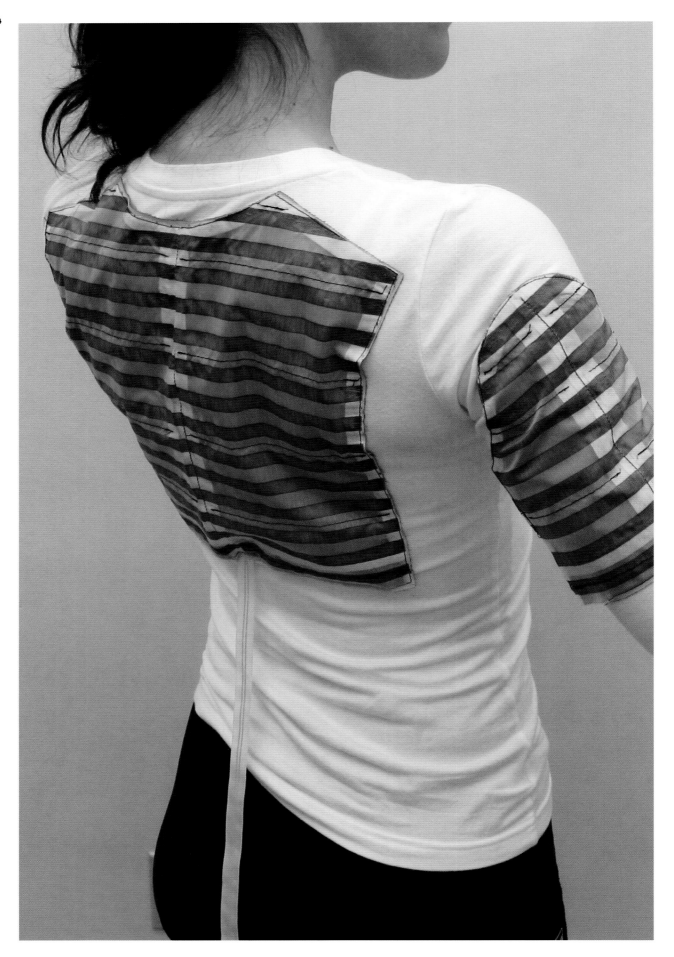

Active agent emerging from iLoad® donor layer

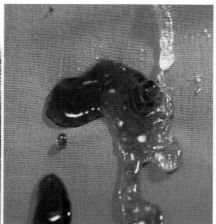

iLoad

Schoeller's iLoad textile substrate can be impregnated with medicines and therapeutic substances that will be absorbed transdermally (through the skin) slowly and evenly over time, and the textile can be replenished when the substances have been depleted. Release is triggered by body heat and perspiration. Developed for medical and sportswear markets, iLoad is now gaining currency among consumers who wish to impregnate it with regenerative substances, such as anti-ageing products, stimulants, relaxants and mood enhancers.

NanoSphere

Coatings and finishings developed by nanotechnology create surfaces so finely structured that few molecules can adhere to them. Some plants have slick, self-cleaning surfaces from which dirt and dust roll off, enabling them to transpire normally and remain healthy, and Schoeller's NanoSphere coatings mimic these surfaces. Clothing that can repel dirt and water in this manner will effectively regenerate itself, remaining clean for as long as its coated surface remains active. NanoSphere coatings share characteristics with P2i (page 116), but are longer-lasting and able to withstand numerous washing cycles without compromising comfort, drape, feel or breathability.

Vitaminized textiles

Japanese fabric manufacturer Fujibo has developed a fibre coated with a substance containing vitamins that will be absorbed into the skin. Made into such fabrics as vitaminized V-Up, the fibres can continue to deliver vitamins transdermally for more than thirty washes. The fibre can be woven into almost any fabric and made into underwear, outerwear, nightgowns and pyjamas.

CHARLES SPENCE

Multisensory materials (that engage several of our senses, such as touch, sound and smell) and tactile surfaces are of particular interest to neuroscientist Charles Spence, professor of experimental psychology at Somerville College, University of Oxford. His research is mapping out how the brain processes the information from each of the different senses in order to form the multisensory experiences that fill everyday life. As Spence calls for a radical re-evaluation of the senses, he reveals that having an awareness of how they influence brain activity can have big implications for the methods designers employ and the ways in which consumers choose and use the products they buy. Applied to clothing, this knowledge enables fashion companies to gain a better understanding of how humans relate to the clothes they wear, the fabrics from which these garments are made and the branding campaigns that promote them. Armed with such knowledge, designers can create clothes that more effectively stimulate the senses, enhance mood and boost performance.

How can knowledge of sensory perception influence the way in which garments are created by the designer and experienced by the wearer?

I guess the key thing is that my research aims to take people away from the focus on the purely visual, and in the case of garments, the haptic and the tactile. Our perception of clothing is far more multisensory than any of us realize. Even when we think we are feeling our clothing with our skin, our perception of it is also influenced by the sounds we hear when we rub fabrics together or against other surfaces, such as skin. Likewise, our perception of something as simple as the colour white is also multisensory, heavily influenced by smell: just add the right fragrance to the wash and people will swear that their clothes look whiter.

Can multisensory thinking help to form lifelong associations between fashion labels and their customers, and to reinforce brand values?

Yes, they can. For example, case studies have revealed how touch and smell create lasting associations. Many children demonstrate an inordinate fondness for their comforter or cosy blanket. What is it about the smooth touch of the trim on such blankets that appeals so strongly to the child that he or she actually bonds with it? Children are forced to grow out of this attachment, but what if we could transfer that inordinately pleasurable and close bonding with an early comfort object to some other item of clothing? It could create a lifelong attachment.

Olfaction (the sense of smell) is equally powerful in its ability to take us back to our childhood. Scented clothing (assuming you have the technology to lay down long-term olfactory cues or refresh them) could achieve this and help to reinforce brand associations as a result.

How can the senses be used to engage and entertain fashion consumers creatively and intelligently?

There are many approaches. Consumers might like unusual experiences – for example, being able to create sounds by the movement of the garments they wear. Something like a swishy skirt that makes more noise than traditional skirts engages the senses more than would a conventional garment.

Designers could be made aware of the fact that the skin is our biggest sensory organ and is linked to states of arousal, and that clothing has more contact with our skin than any other product. Exploiting this would enable fashion companies to stimulate our emotions, and would give them the potential to deliver beneficial health effects, through such devices as aromatherapy or the massage shirt. Note also that garments that feel nice against the skin have the potential to put wearers in a better mood than if they were wearing something that didn't feel so good.

If clothing could interface with the senses, could it reveal our mental and emotional states?

There seems to be the potential for smart fabrics to detect and amplify our internal state – for example, blushing when the wearer blushes. There is already some evidence that people choose fragrances to wear that seem to amplify their own immune system profile. Of course, many involuntary signals sent by the body, such as a change of scent or skin tone, goosebumps and raised hairs, are masked by clothing, so garments that sense those reactions and respond to them would say a great deal about what the wearer was feeling.

Do you think that future garments will contain multisensory technologies?

The drive to make clothing more multisensory has been out there for at least a hundred years, but it seems that now its time has really come. The Italian poet Filippo Tommaso Marinetti, one of the Futurists, had ideas about it in the early twentieth century, but did not have the technology to carry these ideas out. Now designers have the technology they need, yet are still not aware of just how multisensory our perception of the world around us really is.

I would argue that you need the latest in psychology/neuroscience experiments really to bring home to people that how they feel involves not only touch, but also hearing, smell and vision, and that what they see, and how they respond to it, is typically influenced by what they happen to be smelling, hearing and feeling. My research shows that there is the potential for designers to start thinking about all the senses as being more congruent, and when they do, they will be able to design experiences, as well as products, that more effectively stimulate the senses, and hence the minds and bodies, of fashion consumers.

The multisensory world
envisioned by Charles Spence
meets the tactile materials
preferred by Shao-Yen Chen
in this richly textured
garment from the Taiwanese
designer's Autumn/Winter
2011–12 collection.

MARIE O'MAHONY

Irish writer, consultant, academic and researcher Marie O'Mahony's knowledge of materials is vast. Currently professor of advanced textiles for fashion design at the University of Technology, Sydney, she also works across a wide range of industries and market sectors, matching her materials expertise with her knowledge of product performance. Her knowledge in the field of advanced, innovative and sustainable materials has enabled architects, designers and manufacturers to create the products of tomorrow, today. O'Mahony's clients include performance sportswear brands, such as Nike, and such forward-thinking fashion designers as Hussein Chalayan. Her trend research has resulted in exhibitions, such as *The Fabric of Fashion* in 2000–2001 and *TechnoThreads* in 2009, and books, including *Techno Textiles* (1999) and *Techno Textiles 2* (2005), both co-written with Sarah Braddock Clarke (see page 90), and *Advanced Textiles for Health and Wellbeing* (2011). Here O'Mahony considers the role that materials will play in future fashion, and describes how fabric is beginning to bridge the gap between science and design.

How is materials science influencing the way in which garments are created by the designer?

There is a long history of materials research that started in the science laboratory before finding its way to fashion. Historically, these developments came from the fields of space, military and medical research, and it could take twenty to thirty years for us to see them in our clothes.

Now there is a much shorter lead time, and researchers are more inclined to work with designers at an earlier stage in the process. Collaborations between academic researchers, industry and institutions are still complex, but yielding exciting results. The BioSuit, for example, a collaboration between Dava Newman at the Massachusetts Institute of Technology, NASA and Italian protective sportswear firm Dainese, is a new design for an astronaut's spacesuit that provides enhanced extravehicular activity locomotion and life-support systems. It's a great design concept that none of the partners would have developed individually.

Will shape-shifting materials, colour-changing surfaces and wearable sensors be characteristic of future fashion?

Absolutely. These technologies are available now, but not widely used. However, the issue with the greater use of sensory textiles [see page 120] is a design question – why aren't they more widely used? In the 1990s, we saw the thermochromic T-shirts that responded to changes in body temperature. Today we have sportswear and leisurewear that utilize these materials but not in a game-changing way. The development of sensors for clothing made for health-care monitoring and the elderly is of

great importance. This is where I believe we will see some of the first sensory textiles used in the future.

Are fashion designers likely to develop their own materials in the future?

They are already doing it today – for example, the British fashion and design company Eley Kishimoto, in which Mark Eley, who comes from a textile background, and Wakako Kishimoto are both engaged in the development of the garments and the materials used, and Spanish fashion designer Manel Torres of Fabrican, who has developed his own material in the form of his 'fabric in a spray can' technology. In this instance, the material and the garment design are progressing together by necessity.

Will sustainable materials be labelled in the future?

Increasingly, fashion brands want to be perceived as sustainable and ethical. Fabric is central to this, as it touches on so many areas associated with both sustainability and ethics, ranging from producing fibres in an ethical way to minimizing the carbon footprint of the material, coating, finishing and reuse.

The industry is moving towards a 'transparent' supply chain in which the designer as well as the retailer and the consumer can be assured that the garment has been produced in an ethical and sustainable way. We are starting to see a move in this direction, but the development of a suitable labelling technology will really make this happen in the future.

How will today's fabrics be engineered for use by future designers?

We are experiencing a period of great challenges and excitement in materials development for fashion. Smart materials and systems are finally becoming technically and economically more accessible for fashion. Wear and washability are finally being addressed, as is the energy supply necessary to provide power to wearable technology systems. Fashion designers now have the challenge of working out what to do with these technologies that will take them to the next level.

Another area that is starting to come into its own is biomimetics – extracting good design from methods and systems found in nature. We are at the edge of this area from a textile materials point of view. We need to get beyond the coating and finishing treatments and to develop new structures that look and behave differently from anything else. It is more than sixty years since George de Mestral invented Velcro. I want to see more developments that turn everything that we thought we knew about fabrics on its head. Is that too much to ask?

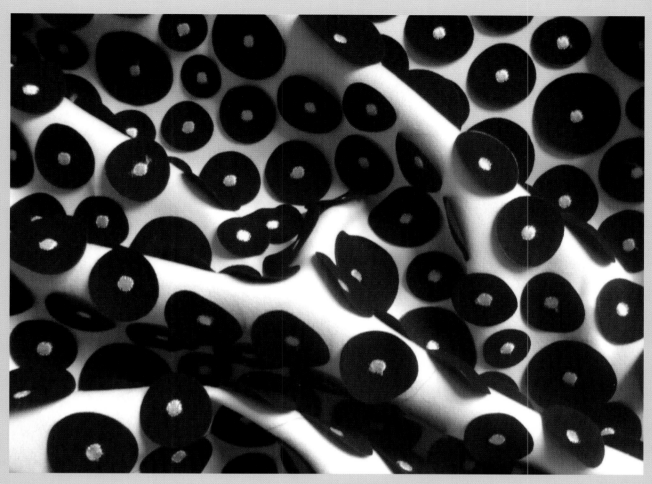

ABOVE
Laser-cut fabric discs were
stitched to this material by
Swiss textile manufacturer
Jakob Schlaepfer. This bringing
together of high-tech processes
and traditional craftsmanship
is a trend championed by
Marie O'Mahony.

RIGHT
Participants in the upcycling
project carried out by surf brand
Rip Curl and Marie O'Mahony
at the University of Technology,
Sydney, found new expressions
for neoprene pieces extracted
from discarded wetsuits. The
piece shown here demonstrates
that new forms can be created
from textile waste.

FUTUR
FABRIC

CREATIVE COLLABORATION
FASHION FROM THE INSIDE OUT
NOVEL MANUFACTURING
VIRTUAL DESIGNS
FASHION AND IMAGINATION
CLOTHING AS SHELTER

Interviews with
SABINE SEYMOUR
SKIN GRAPH

E
ATION

New production processes are bridging the distance between design and manufacturing, and the industry is taking heed of the practical, ideological and multifunctional dimensions that govern fashion

Fashion is beginning to forge fresh markets for itself, and, as a result, entirely new sets of parameters prevail. As designers compete to find ways to ensure that garments fit better, the labels behind them have to invest in expensive body-scanning technology, as well as find the means to coax consumers into using these clothes. Fashion manufacturers can equip clothing with wearable communications technology and climate-control materials, but need technology experts to fabricate them. Some apparel can diagnose the wearer's ailments and medicate through the skin, yet, so far, only medical scientists can engineer them to perform accurately.

Such innovations promise to change the ways in which fashion is designed and consumed, and their impact on manufacturing processes will be considerable. Few are within reach of consumer markets today, and many may take several decades to realize. As the fashion industry starts to upgrade its manufacturing capacity, paradoxically, it is also finding ways to downsize it. Buying digital patterns on the internet, rather than ordering the garments themselves, means that the consumer is responsible for the fabrication of the clothes, and if the patterns are downloaded into a 3D printer (see pages 144 and 148) the items can be made even by people who don't know how to sew. Self-generating fabric can be sprayed on to the body from an aerosol can to create 'second skin' garments (see photographs on pages 146–47), while reclaimed and 'upcycled' clothing creates secondary markets that bypass fashion manufacturing altogether.

The advent of co-creative fashion forums means that the consumer can have direct input into a garment's design, finishing and fabrication. Personalized prints, custom logos and style-specific parameters can be tailored to suit individual tastes. 'Crowdfunded' fashion labels, a system whereby customers are able to invest in the brand and have a say in its activities, enable people to express views about upcoming designs and even the processes that will be used to fabricate them. Fashion is influenced by the global economy as much as by methods of mass production; crowdfunded labels that have investors worldwide benefit from a global input.

Crowdfunded fashion and co-creative platforms inadvertently create forums where traditional ideas about clothing construction can be challenged and discussed. While it may seem progressive to give consumers greater input into the products they buy, their views might not necessarily lead to better products. If designers are overruled, fashion design risks being governed by amateurs. Some people believe that putting their own stamp on garments and accessories makes the item bespoke, but confusing the co-creative process with the time-honoured traditions of Savile Row tailors and Paris couturiers threatens to undermine the legacy of custom-made clothing.

New fabrication methods are bridging the distance between design and manufacturing. As these new methods progress, the industry is taking heed of the practical, ideological and multifunctional dimensions that govern fashion, while at the same time allowing the consumer to experience them in a more creative way. Fashion is becoming multidimensional in form and content, helping to make it an agent of social change and a means of finding personal fulfilment.

OPPOSITE
The individual human voice is as distinctive as a person's DNA, and can be translated into algorithms that encode it mathematically. The 'voiceprints' created through software developed by Australian digital artist Pierre Proske result in unique patterns and shapes that can be printed on to fabric, allowing individuals to create exclusive personalized motifs.

PAGES 134–35
Garments in Dutch designer Pauline van Dongen's Stereopsis collection for Autumn/Winter 2011–12 were fabricated by laser-cutting leather and silk to craft three-dimensional surfaces. Light and shadows animate the garment's surface as the wearer moves, making it appear to acquire new textures and motifs.

CREATIVE COLLABORATION

In years to come, the current decade may come to be characterized by a culture of self-reliance. Banks have long encouraged us to withdraw and pay in our money at cash machines rather than interact with cashiers, and now supermarkets ask us to scan and bag our own grocery items. We book flights online and even check ourselves in before we get to the airport. Today we are being invited to customize our own garments, and even to make them ourselves at home.

One of the first upmarket fashion brands to encourage people to fabricate one of their designs at home was Sans, a small New York label with a worldwide following. When it sold out of its Square Shirt, a lightweight summer top designed in a simple cut, the brand released the garment's pattern to customers online. After paying for the pattern and downloading it digitally, people can cut and sew their own shirt. So that customers could authenticate the garment, Sans sent them an original label by post that they could sew into the shirt.

Downloadable patterns bought direct from fashion labels are sometimes customizable and can be accompanied by online tutorials, appealing to consumers who like to make things, and the system gives people the opportunity to source a design online several seasons after it has disappeared from the shops. Although relatively few shoppers are likely to sew their garments themselves, many would like to have creative input into and to customize the clothes they wear.

Among fashion companies that cater to this wish is the American firm Indi Custom, which offers a selection of jeans cuts, including figure-hugging skinny designs and classic styles. Customers first browse and choose from a range of cuts, types of

LEFT
Indi Custom's clear graphics and step-by-step design options make it simple for individuals to create their own jeans, which are then made up to their specific measurements.

BELOW
London-based fashion designer Helen Storey and Belfast-based textile designer Trish Belford teamed up to create a range of 'catalytic' clothing. The dress pictured here, shown at the Ulster Festival of Art and Design in 2011, can filter pollution, making the air around the wearer cleaner.

Every aspect of a shoe can be customized on Shoes of Prey's website: basic style, type and height of heel, materials, colours and detailing. Once the company has received a customer's specifications, the shoes are made up by hand.

fabric and leg styles; they can move on to select from more than thirty different options for back pockets, then opt for such finishes as sanding and distressing treatments. Indi Custom's proprietary design program asks customers to input their height, weight, and waist and inside leg measurements, and to describe their overall shape, then uses algorithmic software to create customized patterns for them. The specifications are sent to the manufacturer, where the fabric is cut and sewn, and the jeans are despatched to the customer.

A similar methodology is followed by Shoes of Prey, an Australian online shoe retailer that invites people to design their own shoes, and then handcrafts them to match their requirements. Shoppers choose the shoe style, heel height and type, colours and detailing, as well as the materials. Both Shoes of Prey and Indi Custom will make adjustments to the items if they do not fit as well as expected.

Other accessories brands, such as Connecticut-based handbag manufacturer Elemental Threads, have been established to meet the demand for customizable fashion. Elemental Threads gives its clients more than 60,000 options from which to choose in order to design their own handbags. Online design tools take the customer's choice of style, fabric, fastening and lining, and assemble them into a digital image. Orders are sent to the workshop, where they are crafted by hand before being despatched to the customer.

Although ordering goods online depersonalizes the shopping experience, it offers shoppers some of the most affordable personalized goods in fashion today. Part of the consumer need driving customized clothing and accessories is the trend to appreciate craftsmanship and

rediscover the experience of making things.
For most of the past century, mass-production
has been the best business model because it
streamlines production and makes efficient use
of manpower. With the digital design tools and
rapid manufacturing processes evolving today
come financial benefits, and as advanced
technology makes more efficient use of resources,
it can also make each end product unique. New
business models indicate that it pays to give
the consumer a say.

　　Shoppers who prefer manufacturing processes
that reclaim discarded clothing and recycle textile
waste are often drawn to 'upcycling' (a word coined
by William McDonough and Michael Braungart in

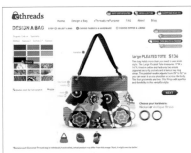

LEFT
Online handbag manufacturer
Elemental Threads meets the
demand for customizable
accessories with a range of
more than 60,000 options from
which customers can design or
personalize their bags.

BELOW
When New York fashion label
Sans sold out of its Square
Shirt (far left), it made the
pattern available online to
customers who wanted to cut
and sew their own top. For that
authentic touch, Sans then
sent them an original label.

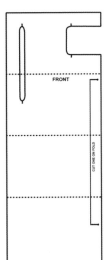

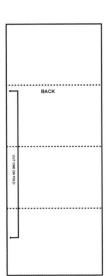

BELOW
Skin Graph's parametric design system (see page 166) scans the body to determine its size and shape, but also detects the individual's range of movement and normal posture. The data is used to create a garment that fits well and moves with the wearer like a second skin.

their book *Cradle to Cradle*, 2002). Upcycled fashions are mostly second-hand or vintage items that have been processed in order to reintroduce them to the top of the consumer goods chain. New Zealand web-based business Carmen Couture reclaims dresses that have vintage appeal and enables people to customize them in order to design their own dresses. Customers choose a vintage garment they like, then open an online template that prompts them to select a bodice shape, skirt style, hemline and sleeve length, as well as buttons, trims and other embellishments. The requirements are sent to the workshop, and a dress is collected from the warehouse and altered to the customer's specifications, then despatched

by post. Thanks to this process, people can reclaim dresses that might otherwise have become textile waste, and restyle them to their own preferences.

Customizing our clothing is about more than simply being able to order a unique garment or ensuring that it has a custom fit. Engagement with the design and production processes boosts our sense of self-reliance, giving us real input into clothes that we wear. Personalized prints, custom logos and style-specific parameters appeal to the wannabe fashion designer within us, and help us to recover some of the skills we will need in order to keep pace with fashion as it moves swiftly ahead.

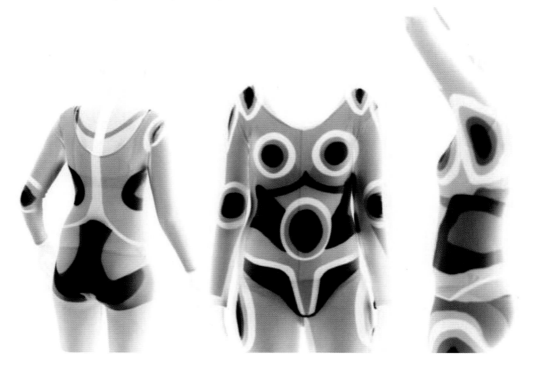

FASHION FROM THE INSIDE OUT

Collaborative fashion designs are redefining the relationship between garment and designer, and challenging the assumption that a garment should be completed by anyone other than the wearer. Customized clothing will be popular among mainstream consumers, but hardcore fashionistas will want to style themselves in wholly unique creations, perhaps even taking fashion to extremes in order to do so.

Beyond aesthetic trends and the practicalities associated with creating unique looks, personalized designs will give fashion more meaning. One-of-a-kind jewellery that replicates the wearer's birthmarks or scars, for example, or those of a loved one, are intended to be symbolic. Such designs can be ordered online from the American label It's My Scar. The first piece of jewellery the company produced was based on a cancer survivor's post-operative scar, and celebrated the wearer's survival with a life-affirming accessory that commemorated the successful end of a long medical ordeal. Today the company creates bracelets, rings, earrings and necklaces based on photos sent in by customers.

Not only can live tissue be a source of inspiration, but also it has the potential to become a future fashion material. Bioscience 'grow-your-own' initiatives show the extent to which active membranes, live cells and human tissue can create wearable forms. Researchers are experimenting with foods and skin lotions that accelerate the growth of certain types of harmless bacteria that line the skin of the human body. If this invisible surface could be combined with bioluminescent agents or reactive pigments, then the wearer's own bacteria could create a garment-like skin.

In another example, designers and scientists are working together to explore how bone-growing

research can be used to create wearable items. Designers Tobie Kerridge and Nikki Stott, researchers at London's Royal College of Art, together with bioengineer Ian Thompson, used live cells from biopsies to form rings that could be worn in the manner of any other piece of jewellery. Early prototypes of this 'biojewellery' were created from osteoblasts, the cells that form human bones, that were grafted on to porous, bioactive ring-shaped forms. As the cells grew, over a period of six to ten weeks they created a structure around the form and replaced it with bone.

So far, the biojewellery venture has generated interest among couples wanting a unique pair of rings made from each other's bone tissue. But bone-growing research is still at an early stage, and growing bone that can sustain itself with its own internal blood-vessel structures may not be possible for some time. Researchers hope that the technique may some day be able to produce large pieces of bone for patients who need bone replacements.

Future fashion designers are likely to promote genetic manipulation techniques as a

ABOVE
In a project created with design agency 125 Creative to 'hybridize science and couture', Nancy Tilbury envisions a future in which the human body can be genetically manipulated to enable fashion and accessories to grow on it, or from within it. Pictured here is the Humanous heel.

OPPOSITE
The Biocouture initiative directed by Suzanne Lee, senior research fellow at London's Central Saint Martins College of Art and Design, explores the potential to grow bacterial cellulose in a laboratory, as if it were a plant or skin, to create a material for clothing. When dry, the bacterial cellulose can be cut and bonded in the same way as most other fashion materials, to form such garments as the indigo-dyed denim-look jacket shown here.

means of styling the body, or to create prosthetic implants that radically alter the body's shape. Such themes underpin the collaborative projects created by Lucy McRae and Bart Hess, a design duo based in The Netherlands. McRae's interest in body manipulation was sparked when she worked on Philips Design's Electronic Tattoo project, which explored how sensing technology could be embedded beneath the skin. The project revealed that fashionistas increasingly see their bodies as platforms for interactive technology, to the extent that some would consider having implants to create changes on the surface of their skin or manipulate their body shape.

Fashion has long been characterized by garments that create new volumes around the body or reconfigure the body's silhouette. Given the current popularity of breast implants, tattooing and cosmetic surgery in general, sculpting the body by the use of implanted devices may not be as radical as it first sounds.

Researchers claim that clothing can be 'grown' from proteins, certain types of fibre and natural cellulose. Future fashions grown from fibres could resemble this dress from Shao-Yen Chen's Autumn/Winter 2011–12 collection, which covers the wearer in varying densities of wool to form different textures.

NOVEL MANUFACTURING

Now that garments can be grown, in the manner of plants, and created by genetic manipulation (see pages 140 and 141), the future of manufacturing processes promises to make them radically different from what they are today. While it may take decades to bring bioengineered clothing to the fashion high street, there are other new and novel processes that will find a market much sooner.

Self-replicating technology makes it possible for individuals to manufacture a wide range of products, including fashion items. Rapid prototyping machines and 3D printers can be owned by individuals and linked to their home computer. One of the first companies to apply the technology to fashion was Freedom Of Creation (FOC), an Amsterdam-based research lab that uses 3D printers to create garments and fashion accessories. These printers deploy panels of inkjets to spray liquid materials that create layers as they dry. As the layers bond and build upwards, they can create flexible membranes, solid forms, objects within one another and objects comprised of interlocking forms.

FOC developed 3D printing technology that mimics loose weaves and chain mail, which it has used to create garments and handbags. In the future, shoppers may be able to buy 3D-printing patterns online and download them, as they can the Sans Square Shirt pattern (see pages 136 and 138), and print the garments or accessories on a replicating device.

Not all fashion designs will have to be paid for. Open-source initiatives make creative content freely available, and open-source communities already share film, music and images today; in the future, this will include a wide range of fashion items and product designs. The downloadable files will enable people to manufacture the objects, and also to

LEFT AND OPPOSITE
Amsterdam-based Freedom Of Creation's 3D printing technology creates chain mail-like fabrics, bags and jewellery. Whole garments can also be printed in 3D, and the technology promises to become more widespread.

PAGES 146–47
Spanish fashion designer Manel Torres has created Fabrican, a unique system of spray-on fashion: an aerosol solution containing fibres that mesh together to form fabric as it is sprayed on to the body. The system works with many different types of fibre, resulting in various textures and properties. Torres, who was inspired by the aerosol bandages used in health care and saw possibilities for a fashion textile that would meet the need for skin-tight tops and second-skin jeans, foresees a day when whole garments will be packaged in an aerosol can and sprayed directly on to the body.

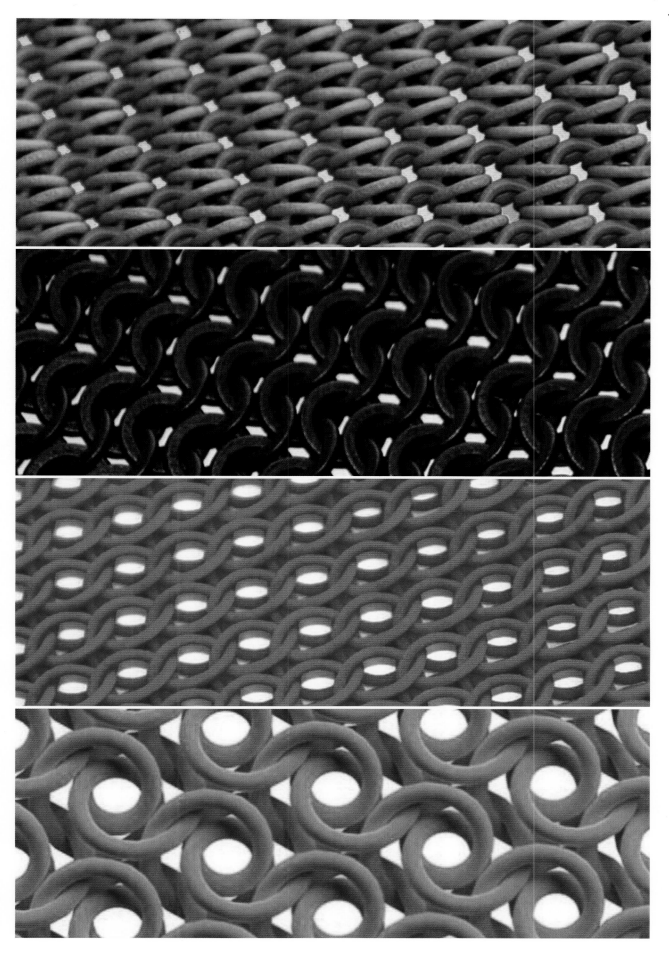

modify them to customize the result. People could then upload their modified version for others to use.

The open-source Fab@Home 3D printer is an affordable, practical means of replicating open-source designs at home, and the range of products it can create includes items containing electrical parts. Soft materials, such as liquid silicone, can be used to produce footwear, accessories and garments, while hard materials, such as stainless steel, can produce such items as jewellery and spectacle frames. 3D printers can manufacture replacement parts too, such as lost buttons, missing clasps and broken zips.

Not all 3D printers have to be bought ready-made: the RepRap open-source project (the name is a shortening of 'replicating rapid prototyper'), initiated by Dr Adrian Bowyer, senior lecturer in mechanical engineering at the University of Bath, has resulted in self-reproducing 3D printers; these can fabricate their own components, which can then be assembled.

Open-source systems represent a new type of business platform, in which ownership of ideas, copyright and other intellectual property rests with the community of users rather than with the originating individuals. Crowdfunded business models operate along similar lines, in that those who buy the 'product' are entitled to 'own' a share of the organization. Crowdfunded initiatives have been popular among independent film-makers, artist collectives and sports teams for some time, and are slowly beginning to have resonance with fashion brands.

Nvohk, a Los Angeles-based surfwear-inspired fashion label, was established as a crowdfunded enterprise. The founders recruited 5000 members, or 'owner managers', who each contributed $50 a year. In return, the members were given a voice in the label's activities, and their input shaped the choice of clothing styles and advertising campaigns launched each season. In addition, they received discounts on what they purchased, and a percentage of the company's profits in the form of reward points that could be used to buy Nvohk clothing.

The crowdfunded approach taken by Nvohk holds appeal with consumers outside the United States, attracting members from all over the world. Along with open-source systems, which gain content from users worldwide, crowdfunded businesses reveal how globalization and the internet are changing fashion at all levels.

BELOW
The latest addition to the Fab@Home series of 3D printers is the Model 2.0 printer, shown here. Whereas earlier models can fabricate goods in plastic materials only, this model's interchangeable tool heads enable the machine to produce objects from a wider range of materials, including fibres.

OPPOSITE
Iris van Herpen has been acclaimed for creating the silhouettes of the future, and her collaborations with architect Daniel Widrig and digital manufacturer .MGX reveal that her 3D-printed designs also herald future fabrication methods.

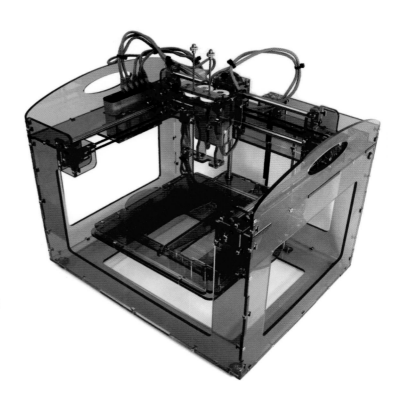

VIRTUAL DESIGNS

Tailoring has undergone dramatic changes in recent decades, but until now nothing in the field has been as radical as body-scanning technology. Whereas tailors and dressmakers may spend hours measuring clients to create a perfect fit, a scanner can sweep over the body in seconds and quickly produce a true-to-scale virtual model. Just like a tailor at work, body scanners determine precise body measurements, recommend appropriate garment sizes and command other manufacturing systems to make customized garments. Some can create a virtual representation of clothing on the 3D model they created, showing the client what the garment will look like when worn.

Although body scanners are new to fashion, they have been used in other fields since the 1990s. Body-imaging technology is replacing conventional security scans in airports, sweeping the surface of the body to look for objects hidden beneath the wearer's clothing. In the sports industry, trainers scan professional athletes to monitor their body shape as it changes throughout training regimes, helping them to enhance their performance. The military was the first to use body scanners to determine garment size, and they proved to be a quick and efficient method of determining the correct uniform size for new recruits. As the technology spreads to the fashion industry, garment manufacturers have been installing full-body scanning systems in such places as shopping malls, boutiques and dedicated body-scanning centres. The scanning systems are augmented by software that translates body measurements into existing dress sizes, directing consumers to ready-made clothing.

Such fashion ventures as the initiative set up by London-based technology company Bodymetrics

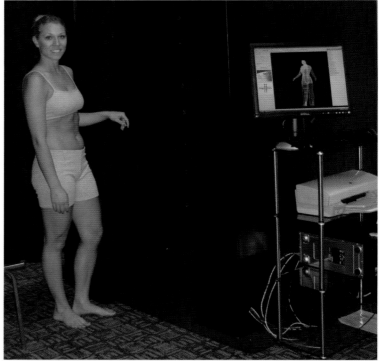

American systems specialist [TC]² designs 3D body-scanning devices for fashion applications. Its NX-16 scanner sweeps over the entire body in seconds and produces a high-fidelity avatar-like three-dimensional model based on more than 400 unique measurements that give a realistic reading of the body's proportions. The scanner can be adapted for use in virtual fashion visualizations, producing links to manufacturers that post 3D digital garments on their websites.

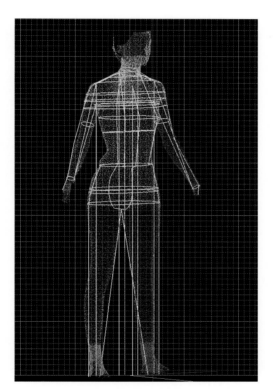

and the American jeans-maker Serfontaine invite customers to be scanned in order to get a custom fit. Bodymetrics has integrated scanning technology into a pod in which shoppers have their exact body measurements recorded. The data is further processed by computer software programs that create a pattern for a pair of perfectly fitted custom-made jeans.

Body-scanning technology can also create accurate, realistic avatars, which are needed to shop for virtual fashion applications. The field of virtual fashion is emerging slowly, but promises to become an important platform in online retailing. The ability to see a scaled model of themselves virtually dressed in different clothing styles is very appealing to consumers. At present, the technology works best with simulations of garment types that fit close to the body, such as jeans, swimwear, sportswear and underclothes. Although it is possible to create simulations of garments that drape, the programming time and the extent of the design work required make it difficult to achieve for a reasonable cost.

It takes just seconds to create an avatar from a body scan. A mesh-like template is morphed with the body scan, the two meeting mathematically as they intersect at thousands of individual points. The resulting figure can be manipulated further by computer modelling programs capable of refining facial features. When complete, the avatar is launched in an open-source format that can be imported into numerous 3D applications, including Autodesk 3ds Max (previously known as 3D Studio Max), Rhino 3D, Maya and other applications that support the standard 3D-object .obj file format.

Users of virtual worlds accessed via the internet, such as Second Life and Entropia Universe, interact with one another through avatars. Virtual goods are designed and manufactured on the sites, where they can be bought, sold, exchanged and hired. The site's users can buy clothing and fashion items for their avatars at 'inworld' stores, along with a wide variety of other virtual goods, and can even design and create 3D garments for them via the sites' 3D modelling tools. These garments often reproduce those found in the real world, altered to create alternative colourways or motifs, or to appear more flattering on the avatar's body than they would on the real person.

Fashion's foray into virtual domains signals a shift in the way in which clothing is produced and consumed. Software programs make it possible for people to create virtual clothing without having any knowledge of fashion design, and are blurring the boundaries between designer and consumer. By moving into a virtual space, fashion is not merely simulating garments that exist, but also creating objects that challenge perceptions of what can be considered to be fashion.

Iris van Herpen's Crystallization collection (Spring/Summer 2011) included garments that were complex in design but simple in construction. Plain meshes and stitched loops were used to create extraordinary designs, demonstrating that striking silhouettes can be fabricated from uncomplicated techniques.

FASHION AND IMAGINATION

Fashion labels are image-conscious, and for several decades creating status and prestige has been key to building brand awareness. This is changing today, as consumers are less likely to buy into status and more inclined to spend their money in ways that make them feel valued. Human attention is the principal currency today, and customers look for experiences that make them feel appreciated by the label they are buying.

In his book *Lovemarks: The Future Beyond Brands* (2004), advertising guru Kevin Roberts, CEO of Saatchi & Saatchi, wrote: 'Human beings are powered by emotion, not by reason.' Roberts advocates a new way of wooing consumers, encouraging brands to foster loyalty among their customers, ideally to the extent that they 'fall in love' with the brand. Many of the top manufacturers and service providers agree with Roberts, but few have been able to figure out how to create lasting emotional connections between their products and the people who buy them. Among those who have succeeded are several fashion labels that have played down status and have instead set about creating loyalty among their customers. These labels want their customer base to remain loyal for life, in the manner of life-long supporters of sports teams.

Younger consumers expect relationships with brands to be based on openness, communication and collaboration, making co-creation with the label a natural choice. The shoe label Dream Heels, based in Winnipeg, Canada, uses its website as a means of communicating with its customers and co-creating with them. Each month Dream Heels holds a design contest, inviting people to submit a design for a high-heeled shoe to put into production. Customers use the site's templates and 3D software to create their designs, and these are subsequently circulated among the company's 'online community' to be voted on. Creators of winning designs receive cash payments and gift certificates with which they can buy shoes from the brand. Most rewarding of all, the winners have their design produced by a brand they adore, and therefore feel a part of it.

Israeli fashion brand Kisim launched a similar competition, inviting people via its Facebook page to co-design a new leather handbag, in the process using social media to expand its fan base thanks to the appeal of the competition. Kisim's highly informative Facebook page explained the design process, materials and fastenings, and showcased the shortlisted sketches for followers to vote on. The winning design, a brown leather shoulder bag with a divider, two internal pockets and a mobile-phone compartment, formed part of Kisim's CollecTik project (*tik* is the Hebrew word for 'bag').

As in the case of crowdfunded business models (see page 148), with co-creation consumers are given real input into the brand. Although co-creative platforms initially appear to make fashion more egalitarian, in fact the opposite seems to be the case. Experts on consumer attitudes claim that customers of high-end brands and luxury labels are not interested in opportunities to co-create with the brand; what they really want instead is privileged access to the brand.

The Red Rail, an Amsterdam-based fashion initiative, created a fashion brand with an exclusive following, and customers have to meet rigid criteria in order to be able to buy: they have to provide evidence of having donated blood. (Initiated by the Nobel Foundation and sponsored by the DOEN Foundation, the label was established to heighten awareness of the need for new blood donors, and

OPPOSITE AND PAGE 156
The Red Rail fashion initiative, established in Amsterdam, was set up to heighten awareness of the need for new blood donors. The label uses high-end fashion as a means to reach a younger generation of conscientious consumers: only people who can provide evidence of having donated blood may purchase its clothes, which are commissioned from such rising designers as Mirte Engelhard (opposite) and Barbara van der Zanden (page 156).

OPPOSITE
One of the outfits for the Red Rail's 2010 collection; see caption on page 154.

BELOW
Trainers from Jimmy Choo's first sports-shoe collection (2010), launched in London with a 'Catch-a-Choo' treasure hunt played via mobile phone.

recruits them from among the younger generation.) The first collection, in 2010, consisted of twenty unique outfits commissioned from a range of up-and-coming designers.

Luxury labels aren't letting go of their exclusive status, but some are striving to deepen their customers' allegiance to the brand by exploring the potential of gaming (such as online games, clock countdowns and real-life scavenger hunts) to create a loyal fan base. The Japanese arm of high-end British menswear brand Dunhill commissioned media company Hakuhodo to design a simple goal-scoring game that was released in

Japan during the 2010 football World Cup. The game simulated a football match and enabled players to accumulate goals that could be exchanged for virtual goods or the opportunity to buy the official Japanese team tie. It could be played on Dunhill's website, and a QR (quick response) code (see page 192) printed in the company's advertisements could link smartphone users directly to the game.

London-based shoe brand Jimmy Choo launched its first sports-shoe collection in 2010 by using the location-based mobile-phone platform Foursquare to create a treasure hunt around central London. Called 'Catch-a-Choo', the game was followed by players using their mobiles; updates revealed the locations of sample footwear, and players quick enough to get to the site before the shoes were moved on won a pair in the style of their choice. The game was an ingenious representation of the collection's street-style design and creative associations. The sports-shoe line was designed to enable wearers to move through the city quickly (as well as comfortably) on foot, which is exactly what the game required its players to do, making the experience more dynamic and far more challenging than playing a game online.

Games and co-creative designs are good strategies for involving the customers at levels to which they would not normally have access. As fashion companies strive in the years ahead to build relationships and strengthen customer loyalty, they will be likely to innovate at other points in the product life cycle, and to link co-creative initiatives more closely to the brand's intellectual and cultural capital. As in the case of all long-term, emotionally charged relationships, brands will have to nurture and value their customers to keep their custom.

CLOTHING AS SHELTER

Architects and urban planners try to make the relationship between the city's landscape and its dwellers as free of friction as possible. Together they devise schemes to facilitate greater flow of movement, designate comfort zones, create climate-controlled spaces and make public transport as spacious as possible. Despite their efforts, many large cities remain congested and overcrowded, plagued by intense traffic and constant transport delays. Modern travel hubs, such as airports and train stations, teem with human traffic, becoming uncomfortably crowded when delays occur.

Recognizing that architects and planners alone cannot create an urban idyll, fashion designers are now addressing some of the city's shortcomings. Urban dwellers want dynamic, multifunctional clothes designs that can shelter them in inclement weather and keep them comfortable as they traverse the cityscape on foot or commute on public transport. Garments that have deep pockets or roomy compartments make it easier to carry belongings, and even to store things that would come in handy should the wearer experience lengthy delays.

The concept of clothing as wearable shelter was introduced in the 1960s by Archigram, a British architectural group that also designed clothing prototypes. It designed the Suitaloon, an outfit conceived as a portable house, and the Cushicle, an inflatable bodysuit containing compartments for food and drink, a radio transmitter and a television screen. These garments were more akin to modular living pods than to clothes, and they enclosed the body in lightweight, portable outfits suitable for outdoor wear. The impetus to create clothing that mimics shelter lay dormant until Japanese fashion designer Kosuke Tsumura launched his Final

OPPOSITE
Malaysian designer Bernard Chandran is known for his sharp cuts and innovative silhouettes. The designer's Autumn/Winter 2011–12 collection included capes, hoods and wraps that shelter the wearer from inclement weather and cold.

PAGES 160–61
Helen Storey's commitment to making fashion more eco-friendly extends to creating clothes that can clean up the environment around them. The 'air-purifying' jeans showcased in Storey's Field of Jeans installation in 2011 are among a range of 'catalytic' clothing (see also page 136) for which she has collaborated with scientists to create fabric coatings that filter pollution from the air so that it does not come into contact with the wearer's skin.

American performance label JakPak created an all-in-one waterproof jacket, sleeping bag and tent. The garment can be used by backpackers and hikers to provide shelter and warmth, or by urban dwellers seeking added protection in bad weather conditions.

Home collection in 1994. With this collection, which included coats made with pockets intended to contain items that would help the wearer to face the daily challenges of modern life, Tsumura created a wardrobe that incorporated the principles of mobility and autonomy, with potential for shelter and warmth.

Moreno Ferrari, designer for Italian menswear firm C.P. Company, took the idea of wearable shelter to another level in the label's Spring/Summer 2001 collection, which included a range of efficient, multi-purpose garments that transformed into armchairs, inflatable mattresses or tents. Ferrari's garments provided the means to fabricate several other objects, bringing an element of utility and functionality to everyday clothing that had not previously existed in urban fashion.

Transformable designs are now beginning to filter into mainstream fashion, providing practical solutions for a range of day-to-day situations. For example, Seattle-based performance label JakPak recently launched an all-in-one waterproof jacket, tent and sleeping bag. Although it was developed with outdoor enthusiasts, backpackers and hikers

in mind, the garment can provide shelter for city dwellers, too.

As multifunctional, transformable designs become widespread in the future, they are likely to contain personal electronic devices that will require an energy source. Designs made with shelter in mind could include photovoltaic materials that would convert solar energy into electricity. Photovoltaic films that can be printed on clothing, such as those developed by Konarka, would provide a lightweight alternative to batteries. When connected to a power source, transformable garments have the potential to shelter their wearers and offer them many home comforts.

Transformable garments are among the most efficient fashion forms designed today. They imbue fashion with principles of self-sufficiency, provide security and shelter, and maximize the wardrobe beyond its wearable potential. Transformable designs exemplify the changes that are taking fashion radically forward, anticipating consumers' expectations that they will be able to get more out of their garments in the future.

SABINE SEYMOUR

Sabine Seymour is an Austrian designer who has forecast, rather than followed, recent cultural and technological developments that are redefining the function of fashion. Seymour never set out to be a fashion designer per se. She first encountered fashion as a young child in Austria, when watching her grandfather, a professional tailor, and her mother, a trained designer, make clothes. As a teenager, she was surrounded by her mother's fashion magazines, but was more drawn to the Commodore 64 computer she received from her father, with which she taught herself to programme computers and build data systems. In 1998 Seymour established Moondial, a fashion technology laboratory with studios in Austria and New York. She is currently establishing a 'fashionable technology' laboratory at Parsons The New School for Design, New York, which she oversees in conjunction with directing Moondial and fulfilling various consultancy roles. As Seymour gave her answers to the interview questions that follow, she presented a few thought-provoking questions of her own.

Will consumers have more input into fashion in the future than they do today?
Customizing a product by choosing designs, colours and so on is an existing practice for people and will continue in years to come. In the future, some garments will be designed by the consumer and then fabricated according to his or her specifications. I predict, however, that this will remain a small percentage.

Fabricating technologically enhanced fashions is complex, and the degree to which they can be customized will depend on the manufacturer's ability. Some future garments will have modular systems that will allow the consumer simply to attach an item of technology by connecting it to an output or input interface, depending on the garment's functionality.

How will high-tech garments be fabricated in the future?
The majority of 'techno fashion' garments will be produced by specialized manufacturers. The specialization will depend on the complexity of the technology that needs to be integrated into the garment, ranging from digital components to nanocoating. The retail outlets that sell techno fashion could be equipped with 'genius bar' tech-support stations, as in the Apple Stores, to help customers to use these high-tech garments to their capacity.

Some consumers might choose self-assembly methods, provided that they have the time and skills to fabricate garments themselves. However, I believe that a mass-market approach will prevail and provide ready-made products. Customized 3D printing or instant knitting might be made part of the retail experience.

Are you saying that existing fashion factories won't be able to fabricate techno fashions?
The ability to mass-produce technologically enhanced garments relies on creating facilities equipped with certain kinds of technology and equipment that can work with advanced materials at every step of the process. For example, fibres need to be enhanced to make textile sensors, then they should be seamlessly integrated into the garment before it can be assembled by a specialized engineer who can fully integrate the technology and make it operable.

Alternatively, manufacturers could take a modular approach and attach components to the garment and then connect them with conductive materials to create a wearable technical system.

What will spark the development of new types of fabrication facility?
We are not at a stage where we can force things to happen, or really even properly provide answers and explanations about getting a new generation of garments up and running. Right now, experts are at the stage of asking the right questions so that we can fully comprehend the scope of the changes that need to occur. Once the right questions are asked, the solutions will follow.

Here are some of the questions I've raised: Can a consumer buy technical components to be attached to a garment in a clothing store? How could 'interactive' garments be displayed in a store? Is the online store an extension of a showroom rather than a store in itself? What is the required expertise of manufacturers? Can we create fibres that are in themselves 'electronic', rather than attaching electronics

to the fibres at a later stage? Can the wearer generate or harvest enough energy to provide a self-contained power source for an electronic garment? And how do we showcase the benefits of the technologically enhanced garment in a way that is accessible to mainstream consumers?

Is today's system of intellectual property rights and copyright laws likely to be valid in the future?
I believe in the model of open innovation, that creative ideas can be shared openly for everyone to develop in their own way. I consider the expertise of creating technologically enhanced garments, the know-how of materials and supply chains, and the awareness of the implications for the market, to be crucial information for corporations, and they need to be paid for adequately. At the same time, it is important for creators to have access to the new materials, processes and methodologies that are developed by such corporate entities. Safeguarding and restricting access to new techniques do not produce innovation but rather hinder it. Not only is creativity stifled, but also the potential for financial returns of investment to the investors is limited.

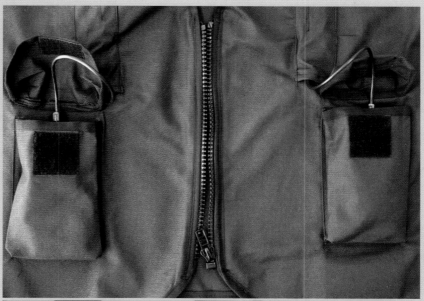

RIGHT, TOP AND CENTRE
Sabine Seymour's Funcl Demo prototype garment is designed to be worn in the aftermath of a large-scale disaster. It includes lighting, GPS technology and gas detectors that can help wearers find their way to safety.

BELOW
Seymour's View jacket prototype, with animated display screens embedded on its surface, could be worn by sports fans to broadcast their loyalty to the team or their favourite players, and even to keep score.

SKIN GRAPH

When fashion designer Laura Michaels and architect Karl Kjelstrup-Johnson joined forces to set up the London-based creative platform Skin Graph, a new system of fashion fabrication was born. Skin Graph's technology uses motion capture and thermal scanning processes to create 3D representations of the body. A parametric modelling program then converts the 3D model into a topographical diagram, which maps out the wearer's contours much as a cartographer would chart a landscape and portray it on paper. The resulting template draws the human body mathematically, representing it as lines, cones, circles and spheres that form the basis of a dress pattern. The pattern is subsequently 'cut' from leather or cloth by lasers, and the pieces can then be stitched or bonded to create a uniquely individual garment. The clothing that results fits the wearer as well as any bespoke garment, moving with the body as though it were a second skin. Here Michaels and Kjelstrup-Johnson discuss how parametric design presents new possibilities for custom-fit clothing, revealing that personalized garments may emerge as the prêt-a-porter of the future.

How does parametric design differ from conventional fashion design?

Fashion designers mostly use traditional tailoring methods, which treat the human body as an object rather than an individual. Tailors take specific body measurements, which don't reflect any feelings or thoughts about the individual, how he or she moves, or how he or she lives. Skin Graph's parametric design technology uses advanced computational strategies so that the individual is scanned rather than measured, capturing a wide range of data that then becomes fabricated as a garment. Our process gives the individual a level of integrated authorship within the design process itself, leading to a truly bespoke garment.

How does Skin Graph create clothing that facilitates the wearer's body movements?

Skin Graph's scanning technology and computational design techniques map out the body on many levels other than shape and size. These multilevel mappings record the gestures, posture and movements of the individual and adjust the design parameters accordingly. The garment is then fabricated according to a 'pattern' that is unique to the wearer. Conventional clothing is made to contain the wearer; Skin Graph's designs are made to move with the body.

Could Skin Graph's design methods be used to fabricate mainstream fashion designs?

They could, and the garments that result would be unique to the wearer. Fashion brands with retail outlets could quickly create a bespoke garment by scanning their customers to make digital representations of them, and then using the data to manipulate a ready-made design so that it will fit them perfectly. Even mainstream fashion brands are starting to see the potential in making virtual versions of their garments for consumers to explore.

There is also scope to use Skin Graph's platform to create virtual garments, which could by tried on by people in a virtual wardrobe. On the other hand, Skin Graph's platform is set up so that it can be used as a tool for providing real-time feedback to the individual. So, the technology could be used to analyse a virtual garment and compare it to the individual's body, helping him or her to decide which virtual garment should be selected and fabricated. This fuses the physical and the digital. Not only will the process create a garment that can be manufactured in the real world, but also it provides an intelligent design tool that acts as a digital signature, which has been tailored specifically for the user, by the user.

How else can Skin Graph have an impact on future fashion?

Skin Graph's design strategy challenges the trend-based fashions that are popular today. Instead of fashion consumers' clothing choices being dictated by the industry, a new model of parametric-design clothing could emerge that is driven by individual styles and performance fits rather than market demands.

Skin Graph's second-skin clothing is uniquely individual. Body-scanning technology maps the wearer's body shape and range of movements, and the fabric is then laser-cut to ensure a comfortable fit. The Skin Graph system can be adapted for use in retail outlets, portending a future method of customizing clothing.

RADICA
RETAIL

SHIFTING SITES
RESALE AND RECYCLE
DIGITAL DRESSING
REMOTE WARDROBES
TAGGING
QUICK RESPONSE CODES

Interview with
ZAHA HADID

L

Fashion retail as we know it today is already exploring a future where boutiques are no longer simply places in which to shop, but are evolving into forums where shoppers can contribute creatively to the brand's output

We do not need to try to imagine the future of retail in order to anticipate the transformations to come; big shifts are already taking place right now. The biggest changes are probably being wrought by consumers, who are beginning to seize control of the fashion system, voicing individual viewpoints and asserting personal power in order to have more input into how and where they buy clothing. Crowdfunded business models enable consumers to buy small stakes in the brand, while initiatives driven by online communities force brands to find ways to reciprocate their customers' support (see pages 148 and 154–57).

Keen to regenerate business in the face of financial downturns, retailers are increasingly aware that they need to build a future based on talking to, listening to and forming relationships with their customers. Future lifestyles will unfold in a culture of communication, collaboration and creation, in which the emergence of partnership branding gives the consumer not only a sense of empowerment, but also a better sense of true value. Many people now want to contribute creatively and feel connected to the products they buy, and they expect the experience of buying fashion to reflect that. So much so that some shoppers consider retail to be an expensive 'middle man' that they can cut out altogether by buying directly from the manufacturer online.

Budget retailers are growing rapidly and will continue to do so, and prestigious brands are following their lead and launching cheaper diffusion lines. The increasing volume of online sales and the success of temporary pop-up shops will cause retailers to question the value of maintaining a fixed, permanent high-street location. Whether based in a physical location or conducting business online, brands will still have to account for the materials they sell and the manufacturing processes they use. Radio-frequency ID tags will make it possible to trace each stage of the garment's production process, distribution and retail sales, while quick response (QR) codes will link real-time shopping with the timeless space of virtual worlds.

Today the distinctions between designer, consumer, stakeholder and shopkeeper are blurring, and they may collapse altogether in the future. As fashion brands have departed from conventional retail, they have established fresh forums that enable them to communicate more effectively with their customers. The sections that follow outline some of the significant shifts now occurring in retail, many of which give consumers a voice in retail's future.

OPPOSITE
Future retail design seems to be polarized. The minimalism of Neil Barrett's boutiques, designed by Zaha Hadid (opposite), is countered by the maximalism of such other shops as London's Dover Street Market (see pages 176–77 and 214–15).

PAGES 172–73
Temporary pop-up shops, such as the Dr Martens pop-up in Spitalfields, London, in 2009, provide fashion brands with an opportunity to test new markets and engage a broader range of consumers.

SHIFTING SITES

Fashion retail as we know it today is already becoming a thing of the past. The industry changed dramatically in the 1990s, when boutiques began to echo the minimalism of art galleries and modernist museums, and even to shadow their geographical locations. Some shops integrated exhibition spaces for contemporary art, or intermingled clothing with decorative items and vintage finds. At the same time, top luxury brands opened shops in run-down but up-and-coming urban areas, contributing to their gentrification. Fashion retail was no longer restricted to the high street, and retail displays were not limited to traditional display methods.

Today, fashion items are as likely to be purchased online as in retail shops. Fashion shoppers flock to their favourite brands' websites, or visit web boutiques that sell a range of labels. At online boutiques, 'e-tail' customers can watch Fashion Week catwalk shows, which were previously accessible only to press and professional buyers. Advertising campaigns are as present on e-commerce sites as they are in magazines and newspapers, and online fashion retail sees as much 'traffic' as the busiest high-street shops. Some designers claim that it is more profitable to exist as a purely online entity, trading via a website without ever having physical retail premises.

The shift to online platforms makes real-world locations less significant, encouraging fashion retailers to try unexpected locations. Many of today's urban dwellers spend more time at airports, gyms and entertainment venues than they do in high-street shops. As a result, clothing boutiques are appearing in cafés, sports centres and other untraditional locations, allowing people to combine shopping with other activities. These days, such places as transport hubs, where people spend time

London's Dover Street Market, established by the Comme des Garçons label and spread over the five floors of a former town house, has an eclectic collection of cutting-edge and leading-edge clothing. The shop's interior fittings and installations change constantly (see pages 214–15) to suit the new clothing styles displayed in the store.

waiting, are as likely to include fashion outlets as food and beverage shops and stalls. Clothes-vending machines, such as those installed in shopping districts by the Reebok and Onitsuka Tiger sports brands, operate around the clock, so that people can buy clothing at any time without visiting any shops. Some fashion boutiques, such as the Happily chain in Japan, are even imitating convenience stores by being open seven days a week and staying open late. The Happily shops also stock a variety of merchandise that a fashion shopper is likely to need out of hours, such as jewellery, tights and cosmetics.

As in the case of fashion itself, clothing boutiques are premised on constant renewal. Over the past five years or so, most major labels have opened at least one 'pop-up' shop, a retail unit open for a limited time in an otherwise unused space. Pop-ups often provide the brand with an outlet in an area where it has not had a presence previously, but they can serve many purposes: they are used variously as outlets for selling discontinued and discounted items, to launch new collections, to communicate something about the label, to generate publicity and to strengthen the brand's profile.

Pop-up shops are popular even among brands that don't already have a retail outlet. For example, online brand Clemens en August, based in Munich, maintains a physical retail presence only twice a year, when it opens pop-up shops in cities around the world, selling its current collection over three-day periods. In a similar vein to the 'trunk show' tradition favoured by American retailers,

who invite designers into their shops to showcase new designs temporarily, Clemens en August has established a platform for reaching new audiences. Rather than describing its strategy in terms of pop-up retailing, Clemens en August considers itself to be simply 'on tour'.

Pop-up shops cut out costly, long-term retail overheads, which, in turn, enables a brand to sell its items at significantly lower prices than it could otherwise. That said, the strategy of short-term retail sales can generate a demand for the clothing based on limited availability rather than price. Some brands capitalize on the appeal, creating limited editions for their pop-up shops and pricing them accordingly.

The success of pop-up retailing has resulted in permanent pop-up venues. Retail innovation consultant Vacant, which reportedly introduced the concept of pop-up retail in about 2005, is currently developing retail venues that can be taken over by a succession of different brands. Its Planeshop concept, a 'rotating' retail unit rented out to brands on a short-term basis, was launched in 2010 at Glasgow Airport; participating brands, which have included K-Swiss and WeSC, take over the store for a limited period, each reconfiguring the unit's exterior graphics to match its identity.

Applied to the high street, the Planeshop concept could potentially renew and revitalize quiet areas. Rotating brands regularly ensures that there's always something new in the shop, drawing more people in as a result. Locating new brands in new sites promises to make shopping more exciting and more convenient in equal measure.

RESALE AND RECYCLE

Fashion retail is most profitable for boutiques that turn over merchandise very quickly. This has contributed to the 'fast fashion' phenomenon, whereby clothes are cheap enough that people can afford to throw them away at the end of the season. As a result, fast fashion is blamed for the unprecedented amount of discarded clothing deposited in landfill. As reported in *The Telegraph* in 2009, it is estimated that in Britain alone cast-off clothing is filling landfill at the rate of more than one million tonnes each year. Some 'lifestyle solutions' and sustainable fashion initiatives encourage fashionistas to cut back on their clothes shopping, and recommend hiring, swapping and recycling clothing as a means of curbing fast fashion. As cast-off clothes are claimed by new owners, they acquire another life, and their extended use reduces the amount of clothing dumped in landfill.

In Australia and New Zealand, high-street clothing retailer Country Road has teamed up with the Red Cross to encourage consumers to donate clothing to the organization's charity boutiques. People who include at least one Country Road garment in their clothing donation receive a credit voucher for use towards their next purchase at one of the label's shops. In Britain, Marks and Spencer has a similar arrangement with Oxfam. Such incentives promise to boost the number of garments donated to these charitable organizations, therefore generating more revenue that they can use for their relief work, and also reducing the number of clothes that end up in landfill.

Swedish fashion brand Filippa K launched a novel means of reclaiming and redistributing unwanted clothing when it introduced the concept of the branded second-hand shop. In Stockholm, customers can return the label's clothing and accessories to the second-hand shop, where the items are cleaned and offered for resale. The initiative reinforces the brand's stated commitment to high-quality, long-lasting materials and its aim of creating classic, timeless styles that remain in fashion for many years. If Filippa K's model takes off, other retailers may encourage customers to return their clothing, and it may be that future consumers will expect to return garments and receive credits for them.

Such concepts of 'life-cycle' clothing are inspiring a new paradigm in clothing retail. The process known as upcycling entails refurbishing discarded items to reintroduce them to the top of the consumer goods chain. As old garments are taken apart and remade, or over-printed with new patterns and surface motifs, they surpass their second-hand status and are accorded the same prestige as new clothes.

OPPOSITE, TOP
Designer Kelsey Ashe, who is based in Western Australia, upcycles textiles and buys new fabrics only from sources certified 'organic'. She also enquires about the working conditions in the country of origin, and refuses to buy textiles from areas where child labour may be used. The garments shown here are from Ashe's Autumn/Winter 2008–09 collection.

OPPOSITE, BOTTOM
Vintage fabrics, textile fragments, nostalgic prints and soft silks come together in Australian designer Sheree Dornan's collections to create imaginary tableaux, as in these designs from her Spring/ Summer 2011 collection that evoke romantic eras and bridge the divide between East and West, history and the present day.

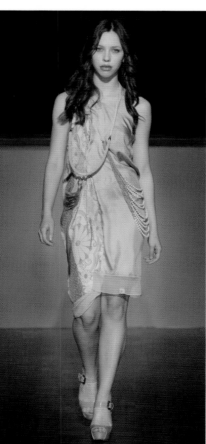

DIGITAL DRESSING

Shopping for new clothes used to include trying them on, but new methods of gauging how well they will fit individual people promise to make the fitting room redundant. Retail shops equipped with interactive software portals can offer shoppers personalized style advice and fashion tips in real time, as can online fashion forums. On fashion websites, virtual fitting rooms enable home shoppers to see how the garments appear on avatar versions of themselves. People linked to social-media networks, such as Facebook and Twitter, or belonging to style-orientated app networks, can upload pictures of themselves and obtain crowdsourced feedback on the garments they are considering buying. Even physical fashion shops are starting to use virtual technology in the fitting room.

In 2010 Japanese cosmetic brand Shiseido installed digital mirrors at its sales points, thanks to which people can try its products without actually applying them to their skin. Customers use the mirror's built-in digital camera to take a portrait of themselves and then scan the bar code of the product they wish to try, triggering the mirror to apply it digitally to their image. A touchscreen interface allows people to select different shades or to source alternative products that better match their skin tone or eye colour. This system provides shoppers with a convenient way to try cosmetics before they buy them and take them home to apply, and developers are currently adapting the technology for use online.

Touchscreen interfaces are being integrated into e-commerce sites to enhance consumer contact. People who have webcams can communicate with e-tailers offering Skype-like video calls, watching a salesperson 'touching' and moving virtual objects much as they would in a

physical store. At the touch of a finger, the salesperson can drag virtual versions of products on to the screen to demonstrate their features, then drag them into the customer's online shopping cart or return them to the shelf.

Physical retail outlets are installing interactive technology in fitting rooms, where it can heighten the experience of trying on clothes. In 2010 global fashion label Diesel piloted the technology in its shops in Spain. Shoppers can take pictures of themselves as they try on clothes, then edit and enhance them before uploading them on to such platforms as Facebook. Shoppers can then benefit from real-time feedback and comments from friends about their potential purchases.

Whereas most fashion websites use touchscreen technology and digital imaging to build loyalty to a particular label, at looklet.com people can browse the season's favourite garments and create new styles for themselves. Although Looklet (which described itself at its launch in 2009 as 'the world's first digital styling studio') does not currently offer a touchscreen interface, it does provide the means to mix and match designer clothes selected by stylists from top fashion labels. Looklet's users choose a model and a backdrop, then browse through some 2000 images of individual clothes and fashion accessories that can be dragged on to the model to dress her. People can experiment with different looks or create a personal style, which is viewable from multiple perspectives; they can save the styles they create, circulate them among other Looklet users and share them with friends on such networks as Facebook and Twitter. Saved styles are easily retrievable, and can be restyled at any time. Looklet claims that in the first two years of the site's existence some 76,000 users created more

Fits.Me's virtual mannequins are in fact a single shape-shifting robotic form able to replicate thousands of different body shapes. Web users input their measurements and select the garments they are thinking of buying, which triggers the mannequin to change shape and show how the items will look on the individual's body.

  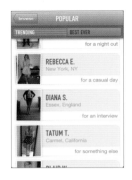 

than 600,000 outfits. A number of similar sites have now been launched, indicating that such forums may be widespread in the future.

The online portal GoTryItOn.com has emerged as a forum where fashionistas upload digital snapshots of themselves trying out various looks in order to get feedback before deciding what to wear. They can list the brands behind each outfit and say whether it is intended for a particular occasion or special event. Others on the site can then vote for or against the look, suggest changes or give compliments. The wearer can later give his or her own feedback, letting others know how the outfit worked out.

Web portals that allow users to mix and match virtual garments encourage fashionistas to shop online because people can create looks they are happy with before they order any clothes. However, some online shoppers find it frustrating that they can't actually try clothes on before ordering, and e-tailers generally experience a high rate of returned goods. Virtual fitting room Fits.Me is a web-based interactive technology that fashion e-tailers can licence in order to enable their customers to see how their choice of garment would fit their body type. Fits.Me's technology produces a virtual robotic mannequin capable of replicating thousands of different body shapes. Shoppers enter their personal measurements

and then choose garments, which morph to show how they will look on the specified body type.

Avatars can simulate an individual's body type perfectly, and in virtual worlds, such as Gaia and Second Life, they can be clothed in the latest fashions. Gaia took a bold commercial step in 2008 when it began selling real-world fashion on its site, enabling its real-life members and their avatars to wear identical garments. Avatar dress-up site stardoll.com is creating new markets for virtual clothing by teaming up with garment manufacturers and e-commerce sites to enable users to make virtual clothes for wear in the real world. Initially users could take only logos or motifs from the fashions worn in the Stardoll world and have them printed on T-shirts, jackets and fashion accessories, but the potential market for real-life avatar clothing among young consumers attracted the interest of manufacturing partners.

The advent of virtual-world clothing being translated into physical-world fashion reveals just how important digital platforms will be in the future. When combined with platforms enabling people to create fresh looks, avatars and other technologies that create virtual versions of the user's body type offer potent alternatives to the hassle of high-street shopping. Whereas real-world fashion once dressed virtual humans, future fashionistas are likely to dress themselves digitally before they consider buying real clothes.

On such online portals as the GoTryItOn.com interactive forum, users receive feedback on the looks they upload, helping them to put together the perfect outfit.

REMOTE WARDROBES

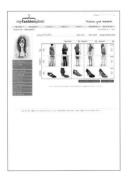

Such online wardrobe management sites as My Fashion Plate provide users with tools that help them to get the most out of the clothing they own, with virtual clothes cupboards, body-shape analysis and style advice from a stylist.

In the future, not all the garments we wear will take up space in the wardrobe. Clothing will be available for hire on terms similar to those of rental cars today, making it practical and affordable to wear the latest styles. Given the rapid pace at which styles change, it's no surprise that consumers would like to avoid the expense of buying clothing and hire it instead, either long-term (for a season, say) or for a one-off occasion.

Clothing hire has existed for a few decades, typically providing clothing for special occasions, expectant mothers and individuals embarked on weight-loss treatments. Clothing hire can also meet the needs of fashionistas who want to vary their wardrobe without investing in new clothes, or who simply prefer not to wear the same garment twice. Web-based hire company Closet Infinite allows its members to hire garments for free in return for donating fashion items of their own. From its offices in Singapore, Closet Infinite recruits members worldwide; potential members submit a picture of the garment they'd like to donate, along with a description of its condition, and say where it was purchased and how much they paid. On acceptance, applicants are entitled to a six-month membership, allowing them to hire the donated clothes of others for free. Members simply browse Closet Infinite's database and select the clothes they wish to hire, then pay the deposit required for the items and a handling fee that includes packaging, postage and cleaning. The garments are despatched by post, and the deposit is refunded when the clothes are returned.

People will continue to store utilitarian garments, such as sportswear and underclothes, at home, but cherished items, vintage styles and collectible garments will be carefully catalogued and stored offsite. Space-strapped urban dwellers would rather not be burdened with possessions they aren't currently using, but the expense of self-storage units and the hassle of getting to them put them out of the reach of most people. American service Storage By Mail offers flexible storage that could help fashionistas pare down their home wardrobe. Customers catalogue the goods for storage online or via a smartphone app, create shipping labels for each item and send in the goods by post. Items can be retrieved at any time, and Storage By Mail guarantees to ship them out the following business day.

Fashionistas who find it difficult to keep track of all the items they own can make it easier by setting up a virtual wardrobe through such online style communities and wardrobe management tools as My Fashion Plate. This was acquired in 2011 by 'fashion community' Club Tutto Mio, and will be undergoing some changes, but in its previous incarnation users uploaded photos of clothes they owned or planned to buy, and the site then offered body and style analysis to determine which sorts of garment best fit the user's body type. Also available were a design-studio tool to create outfits from among the images uploaded, a travel tool for planning and packing the right clothes for a trip, and a budget planner to keep track of clothing costs. Efficient and accessible, My Fashion Plate was even used by professional stylists to keep track of their celebrity clients' wardrobes.

TAGGING

Fashion is full of signifiers. Clothes say much about the wearer's status and style, and the logos, labels and motifs they contain signify the garment's pedigree and worth. The labels sewn into clothes tell what materials they are made from and how they should be cared for. Retailers attach hanging tags that state the size and price, and the bar codes printed on them identify the type of merchandise they are.

In fashion today, the role of tags and the information they contain is changing dramatically. Whereas tags once held only limited information about the garments to which they were attached, they now have the potential to be interactive devices, tracking mechanisms and information portals that link with other merchandise. Electronic tags embedded with radio-frequency identification (RFID) technology use radio waves to transfer data to a reader, making it possible to identify the garments and track them.

RFID technology provides a more efficient method of identifying garments than bar codes. An RFID tag is not scanned by the reader as a bar code would be, so it can be read even while it is inside packaging or shipping containers. RFID tags crafted with a built-in battery or power source emit signals strong enough to be read from several metres away, even if they are not in the line of sight of the reader; those made without an energy source, called 'passive' RFID tags, can be read within close proximity to a reader. And whereas bar codes can be read only one at a time, RFID tags can be read by the hundreds.

The concept of what a tag can convey, and the kinds of item to which it can be attached, has expanded in recent years. Just as a fashion manufacturer can encode RFID tags with shipping data, so individuals can use them to 'tag' pieces with information. For example, in 2010, as part of the Future Everything digital arts festival in Manchester, individuals who donated clothing to an Oxfam charity shop were asked to record brief stories about the garments; these audio clips were linked to RFID tags attached to the clothes. Shoppers could activate the audio files with their smartphone or one of the shop's RFID readers, which relayed the audio files to speakers in the shop. The project brought the clothes to life, revealing that many had a rich history, and in many cases the shopper's decision to buy one of these garments was influenced by the audio clip.

RFID technology can link garments to internet platforms. The web-based platform EmmaActive, developed in Canada, uses tagging technology to create online links to clothing and other products. Images of fashion items can be tagged with the name of the manufacturer, creating a link to its website, and individual images can be tagged multiple times to reveal the name of each fashion label, accessory brand and jewellery design shown in that image. When people click on an item they like, they are directed to the brand's website. Incentives are given to members of the public to identify and tag images of garments they recognize: if the tagged brand is a member of the EmmaActive network, the person who initially tags one of its images receives monetary rewards from the brand every time the tag is clicked in future.

Much online content is linked to real-world objects, and RFID technology can create automatic connections between the two. If RFID tags could be embedded in fashion items, and scanned by such everyday devices as mobile phones and laptops, links to the online content about them would open automatically on people's personal devices as they passed by the pieces. The technology would not be

Hypertag encodes short-range, high-frequency RFID tags with a wide variety of information, and includes links to websites, videos and images. When scanned by a smartphone, the RFID tags link to online content or trigger applications to upload.

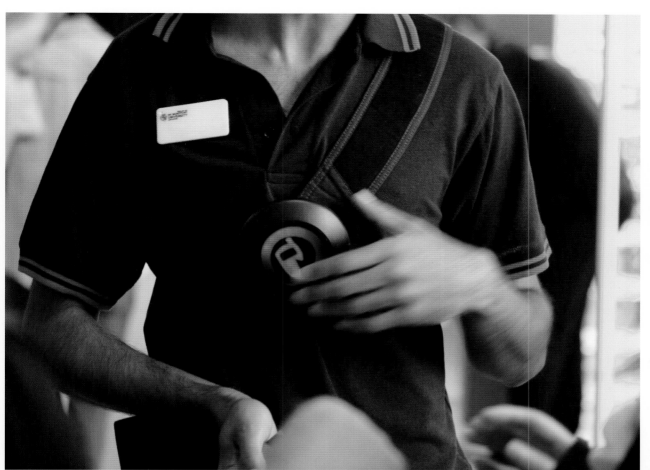

limited to garments and accessories: fashion advertisements, look books, flyers, brochures and product samples could be tagged, too. RFID developer Touchatag (previously known as TikiTag) has created short-range, high-frequency RFID tags that people can scan with mobile phones to link to online content or applications. A portrait of a fashion designer can link to the designer's online profile, for example, or a logo on a shopping bag can connect to the brand's website.

The battery-powered tags created by British developer Hypertag emit infrared signals, and can be embedded in a variety of media and materials, such as billboard advertisements. Hypertags can be easily 'read': people need only point their mobile phone at an embedded advertisement and click 'accept' to download information from the brand's website. Hypertag manages the content (such as images, texts and videos) that the brand links to each tag, and monitors and updates the web pages downloaded via the tag. People's response is relayed to the advertiser, which can amend and update its online information as consumer traffic indicates which areas are of most interest. Hypertag's vision for future fashion retail would include people clicking to download information when they see a fashion advert, then browsing through the collection and ordering the garment in their size.

Tags may also make it possible to locate lost or stolen goods, as RFID readers could be set to scan for items encoded with specific individual identification codes. Such security companies as web-based Bak2u have developed individually encoded tags that people can attach to their possessions. Subscribers register tagged items on Bak2u's website, so that any missing items can be returned if found.

RFID technology can be programmed to scan automatically, and even to trigger other systems to activate when certain parameters are met. Sensors in shop fitting rooms, for example, could scan the garments being tried on and trigger video screens to project images of those clothes being worn by models or celebrities. RFID relays could identify the social-media network apps downloaded on to a shopper's mobile phone, and request permission to activate a web camera that would broadcast images of the shopper online for his or her friends to see. As a result, the brand could interact with shoppers as well as their online social networks, thus widening its reach.

For some time garment manufacturers have been petitioned to use ecologically sound production methods and sustainable materials. These days, they are under pressure to prove it. New standards of accountability dictate that manufacturers will soon have to demonstrate the authenticity of their goods. Within the next decade, fabrics, and hence garments, will be encoded with information about their origins and materials (see, for example, DNAtex, page 115). RFID-embedded fabrics could be encoded with standardized labelling information to ensure that shoppers can trace the provenance of anything they buy. The RFID tagging will be updated at every stage of the garment's production cycle, charting each process the item has undergone. The information encoded into the tags may even make it possible for the manufacturer to identify where any defects could have originated.

The claim that RFID tags will be an efficient, and perhaps necessary, means of tracking garments through the stages of manufacture and transport is contested by such organizations as CASPIAN (Consumers Against Supermarket Privacy Invasion

British charity Oxfam participated in Manchester's Future Everything digital arts festival by tagging donated clothes and accessories with RFID tags that connected to audio accounts of the items' history.

and Numbering). The group warns that RFID devices embedded in clothing could easily link to customers' names and credit-card information during sales transactions, making it possible for retailers, and others, to track shoppers. In an interview quoted on spychips.com, CASPIAN co-directors Katherine Albrecht and Liz McIntyre observe that 'selling a pair of shoes that doubles as a tracking device without telling consumers about the RFID device it contains is essentially a form of fraud ... Once mandatory labelling is in place, if people choose to buy shoes that can track them, that should be their free choice. But consumers must be informed of what that choice means.'

The presence of RFID tags could also raise issues concerning the concept of ownership. Chips embedded in bank cards, for example, remain the property of the bank at all times, irrespective of their being held by the consumer. If this notion were applied to fashion brands, which would want to assert ownership of the embedded tags because of their integral relationship with companies' data systems, it could mean that a garment was merely licensed to the consumer for the duration of its lifespan.

RFID technology and the systems that sustain them are being improved and enhanced all the time. At the time of writing, developers maintain that in the future, fashion companies will be more likely to tag garments with ultra high frequency (UHF) chips, which are considered to be the next generation of RFID technology because they facilitate faster data transfer and longer read ranges than RFID does today. As tagging technology moves forward, developers and legislators are considering issues of ownership and data protection, and are endeavouring to finding viable solutions to these problems.

QUICK RESPONSE CODES

Quick response (QR) codes are almost everywhere, tagging the world around us as they attach to products, advertisements and signs. The simple geometry modules that make up their design, together with their stark black-and-white matrix, give them a graphic quality. They contain more data than bar code, and can be read as easily by mobile-phone cameras as by sophisticated bar-code readers. They can be decoded at high speed, and the information they contain transforms a product into an 'object' that communicates something about itself or the environment around it.

Unlike RFID tags, QR codes do not emit radio waves. They do not resonate with high-frequency signals, and since they need to be visible in order to be read they are unlikely to be embedded in fabric. The QR code originated in Japan in the mid-1990s, where it was created to tag automotive parts. It revealed its potential to say something about fashion when Calvin Klein Jeans posted a large QR code on its billboard ads in New York to mark the launch of its Autumn/Winter 2010–11 collection. Smartphones could be used to scan the code, which featured underneath it the message 'Get It Uncensored'. The QR code triggered the download of a video advertising the collection that people could watch and replay.

Since then QR codes have been seen on a range of fashion items. T-shirts printed with QR codes contain messages about the brand, or reveal a viewpoint or slogan the wearer wishes to share surreptitiously. American web agency Tikaro prints QR codes on badges that can be attached to almost any garment or accessory. The Velcro-backed pieces

of cloth, dubbed 'p8tches', are printed with a variety of designs and a QR code underneath. The code is actually a URL (uniform resource locator) that can be scanned with a smartphone and links to the p8t.ch domain. Tikaro is aiming its p8tches at customers who have a web presence, who could set the redirect target of the URL to their own web page. Fashion bloggers, for example, could redirect the QR code to their blog, where they would upload comments on the garment on to which the p8tch is attached.

QR codes are useful in retail, too, as they enable people to make purchases using their smartphones. In South Korea, they are used by Home Plus 'virtual shops': sales points constructed in the real world but that do not contain any physical products. The virtual shops, located in such sites as subway corridors, are constructed from backlit billboards displaying images of the items for sale. QR codes appear alongside each image, enabling smartphone-equipped commuters to scan the code and add the product to their virtual shopping basket. Items are then despatched to the buyer.

One of the characteristics of QR codes is that they are not traceable in the same way as RFID tags are, thus minimizing the risk of breaching data protection acts or making the shopper a victim of tracking technology. The web links QR codes provide enable them to perform as brand-enhancing signifiers, leading people to interactive, informative domains. As QR codes provide new ways of interacting with clothing, the dynamic experiences they generate pave the way for deeper layers of fashion to surface.

Tikaro's Velcro-backed 'p8tch' QR code pads (above and opposite) are designed to be easy to attach to clothing or accessories, and to transfer to another item.

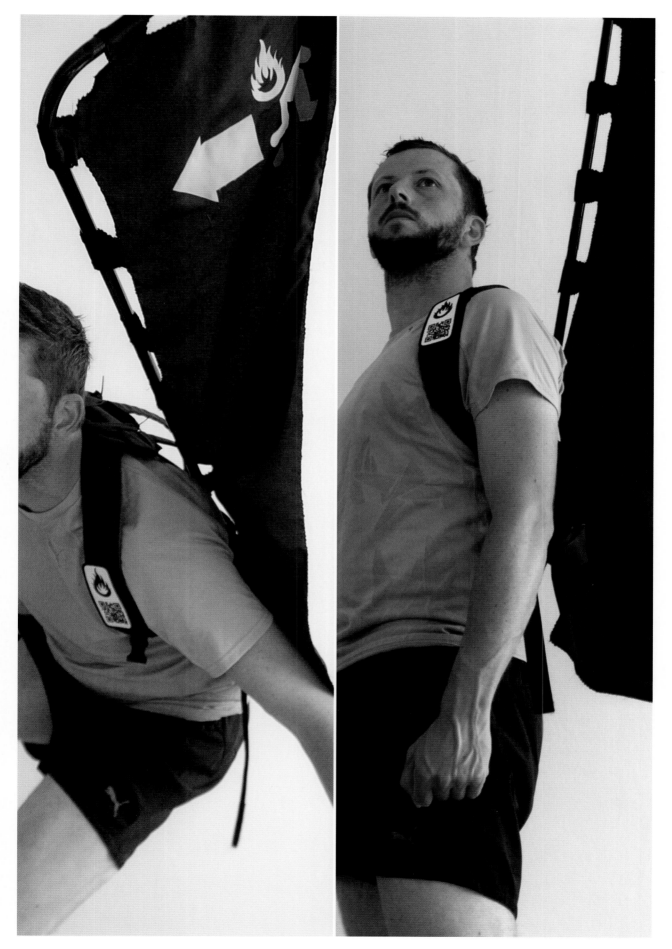

ZAHA HADID

London-based Zaha Hadid is one of the world's most fashionable architects, and she and her team have strong ideas about the synergy between fashion and architecture. Hadid regards the two as components within a single system of design, famously likening the sensual appeal of her buildings to the tactile sensations of wearing a garment. Just as clothing is based on the proportions of the human body and sits close to its contours, architecture is also structured in relation to the human body, which it can contain within itself. When interviewed for this book, Hadid cited fashion designer Neil Barrett's concept store in Tokyo and his other retail boutiques as leading examples of how fashion and architecture are coming closer, and forging new directions for fashion retail.

Can architectural design reflect the style ethos of a designer's clothing?
Yes, it can. Take our concept for Neil Barrett's fashion boutiques as an example: it is based on the minimal cut of the brand's fashion design and it parallels the brand's approach. Neil Barrett produces both menswear and womenswear, so we used characteristics of the male/female dualism to complement and contrast the masculine and feminine designs that will be displayed in the shop.

How is this reflected in the boutiques?
Our design scheme charges the space with imposing objects that engage the customer, and enables people to experience the garments and accessories displayed in the space in multiple ways. For example, the furniture piece on the ground floor of Neil Barrett's Tokyo shop is designed as a strong, masculine and dynamic form, while the piece on the first floor enunciates femininity through more fluid contour lines.

You are designing boutiques for Neil Barrett throughout the world. Is the master architectural design intended to appeal to fashion consumers in so many different cultures?
The design is primarily made to complement the Neil Barrett brand and to create a spatial expression for it. Every single part of the retail design acts as a piece of a puzzle that completes, complements or comprises the other parts. So these pieces can be paired adjacent to each other or separated by distance, and still project the same message. No two boutiques will be identical; each will be tailored to suit local parameters.

In what ways can fashion and architecture come together in the fashion retail of the future?
Fashion and architecture are design interventions that, at their best, come together in fashion retail to create a strong vision and cohesive experience. Fashion and architecture can use the same design parameters of fixed points, folding, pleating and cutting out shapes and spaces. Principles of fashion and architecture can be used to define a single room or space, allowing the customer to experience the space in multiple ways and interpretations.

OPPOSITE AND PAGES 196–97
Zaha Hadid's minimalist designs for Neil Barrett's shops, such as the flagship Tokyo branch shown here, reflect the brand's signature minimalism, showing that fashion trademarks can be represented in architecture to create a closer relationship between retail spaces and the brands that own them. Although Hadid created a masterplan for Barrett's boutiques, no two will be identical; each will be tailored to heighten its appeal to local shoppers.

FUTUR
HORIZ

Interview with
ANNE MARIE COMMANDEUR

E
ONS

**As fashion strives to become more
multipurpose, overlaps with other disciplines
and acquires new functions, it is sparking
new shifts in our expectations of clothes**

Although the future is by definition yet to come, it is inextricably linked to events taking place in the present. Among the developments emerging in the world of fashion today are designs, ideas, technologies and materials that are already creating the styles of tomorrow, and the processes developed to realize them go far beyond addressing aesthetics, comfort and fit. Much emphasis is placed on innovation and performance, which drive the development of techniques that will be needed in order to incorporate seamlessly the devices, media content and communications networks that wearable technology will bring.

As fashion strives to become more multipurpose, overlaps with other disciplines and acquires new functions, it becomes more challenging to chart the developments that result. The following sections identify some of the key directions fashion is taking, and chart how these developments spark new shifts in our expectations of clothes. Some of the developments indicate that consumers will be able to contribute creatively to the brands they buy and to shape their online content, and this direct input will enable the brands to glean information on people's attitudes, expectations and buying decisions at first hand.

With people now able to articulate what they want to buy in the seasons ahead, will the concept of trend, as we understand it today, remain valid? Trend forecasters are aware of the consumer-led initiatives to come, but, understandably, are reluctant to publish projections revealing that their own influence may soon diminish. The new generation of consumers will embrace new styles, but will regard them as being only surface-deep. Although tomorrow's fashion brands will continue to originate new looks, future fashionistas will care less than they do today about how garments appear, and more about what they can help the wearer to achieve.

OPPOSITE
This dress by Shao-Yen Chen anticipates the fashions of the future, when performance and innovation will play more important roles than they do today. Some surfaces will be richly textured, even to the extent that they can change in shape and appearance. With new textures will come the means of keeping fabrics soft, fresh and looking good for longer.

PAGE 202
Sharply tailored suits will never disappear from fashion completely. This trouser suit by Irina Shaposhnikova uses geometric shapes to craft eye-catching textures and a crisp, streamlined silhouette.

PAGE 203
Haider Ackermann cut this sleek trouser suit close to the body and paired it with a billowing cape that creates volume around the wearer. Future fashions will continue to juxtapose these two extremes. As women wear body-conscious clothing, they will also want to cocoon themselves in voluminous silhouettes.

THE END OF TRENDS?

Fashion forecasting is a huge industry. Forecasters predict the colours, fabrics, looks and styles that will influence fashion in forthcoming seasons, and create trend reports that they sell to clients. Trend reports are widespread throughout the industry, influencing designers working in couture, prêt-à-porter, sportswear, street style and mainstream fashion. Advance knowledge of emerging trends helps fashion brands to tailor their styles to suit consumers' attitudes, and even to identify new markets for their merchandise.

Most fashion professionals subscribe to forecasting publications, buy trend books or even commission bespoke fashion concepts from leading forecasters, in the hope that the inspirations and insights they contain will give them a competitive advantage over others in the industry. The reports identify the recurrence of aesthetic cycles, chart patterns in consumer behaviour and make projections that form the basis of long-range forecasts. Forecasters generally claim that when 15–25 per cent of a given population have incorporated an innovation, action or belief into their normal lifestyle, it can be acknowledged as a mainstream trend. Forecasters also recognize concepts that relate to some of the global shifts known as megatrends, which are typically considered to be more long-term and wider-reaching than ordinary trends. Knowledge of lasting trends can help designers to differentiate between long- and short-term trends, and to gauge which sectors of the market they reach.

Large fashion companies often have in-house trend researchers, who work alongside their creative colleagues to source inspiration that will reflect the brand's overall style and to create looks and promotions that typify it. In-house trend research can be applied across the board to all fashion collections and accessory lines, as well as in the production, marketing and distribution of the products – a concept known as vertical integration. A label that has its own retail outlets, for example, is likely to apply information on consumer attitudes to both garment design and point-of-sale merchandising to maximize the synergy between them.

The emerging culture of co-creative design and crowdfunded labels is creating an interface between brands and consumers that enables designers to detect significant shifts first-hand. As input from co-creative consumers is catalogued and analysed in-house, it will spark a shift towards vertically integrated methods. Industry professionals are likely to use online sources to verify the input from their customers, or conduct additional market research to explore further new directions.

The movement to remunerate consumers for tagging merchandise online (see page 188) and broadcasting purchases through social-media networks may soon extend to rewarding brand followers for reporting consumer moods and attitudes. Collecting customer feedback in this way would give brands valuable input from a network of individuals who have a sound understanding of the milieu at which the merchandise is aimed. Consumer input will be given more importance in fashion think-tank forums, where the views of the 'person on the street' will be valued as much as input from experts.

The emergence of the creative consumer will be one of the most significant developments in future fashion. Current perceptions of trends will change as fashion brands look for narratives, 'creative' directions and new platforms. Reassured by their customer base, fashion brands will rely less on trend reports and more on their own creative direction.

Rick Owens's Spring/Summer 2011 menswear collection presented an austere vision of men's fashion that contradicted the season's trends. The collection included efficient, functional and uniform-like garments. Such clothing has been a staple of mens' clothing for several centuries, and is likely to remain so in the future.

FASHION FORESIGHT

Although fashion is characterized by short-lived looks, the industry itself is underpinned by long-term developments that spark new styles and influence their impact. Modern fashion has always reflected societal shifts, financial markets, economic strategies and political affairs, and will continue to do so in the future. Yet, as fashion becomes increasingly multifaceted and begins to interface with more disciplines, its future will be driven by technological developments more than is currently the case. Engineering, biotechnology and scientific research will all have an impact on the way clothing is worn and experienced, while shifts in consumer attitudes will revolutionize the ways in which garments are designed and sold.

Against this background, in order to predict the styles to come, forecasters and fashion practitioners will have to consider a broader range of factors than they do today. Anticipating emerging shifts will not be easy; they may be sparked by developments in one or more of the disciplines underpinning fashion, or result from the synergy between several of them. Fashion designers, having handed over some measure of creative control to the consumers, will be less concerned with creating styles, and more focused on receiving feedback that can help them to make garments more multifunctional. Analysts will survey consumer needs in order to identify areas in which clothing styles can provide 'solutions' to perceived problems, while fashion companies will launch services and amenities that generate more revenue for them than making clothes does. Future brands may even provide concierge-type facilities that rival those of top hotels, offering their services to anyone who wears their label.

The following sections outline some of the directions fashion is taking, identifying key developments that could spark radical shifts in our expectations of clothes. Such insights may help practitioners to anticipate some of the innovations to come, and even to draw strategic conclusions about the steps to be taken right now.

Predicting the trends to come is never easy, as current forecasters take into account colour combinations, textile trends, market shifts and emerging consumer needs. In the future, technological innovations will also be a consideration, as garments become equipped with wearable software. Pictured here is one of Philips Design's outfits exploring 'emotional sensing' to demonstrate how electronics can be used to express the emotions and personality of the wearer.

CONSUMER CLOUT

As fashion consumers contribute creatively to collections and support crowdfunded brands, the balance of power between customer and company will shift dramatically. Loyal shoppers will be rewarded for boosting the brand's sales through their use of social-media forums and professional networks.

'Cash in' consumers

Social-media forums and interactive networks will dramatically boost retail sales, and fashion consumers will want a piece of the action. Some brands are gearing up to offer monetary incentives or other rewards for online tagging (see page 188). Having realized the value of consumer feedback, brands will ask customers to make reports on emerging trends and identify promotional opportunities, and will remunerate them accordingly. People will readily participate in co-creative design forums, but, despite emerging open-source platforms (see pages 144–148), they will want to copyright their ideas in case the brand decides to commercialize them. Members of the public will be lured into believing that their co-creative design could be the next big thing, but when it comes to tapping consumers for help, no one will profit more than the brands.

Co-creative design

Personalized prints, custom logos and style-specific details appeal to consumers who want to rediscover the experience of making things. Digital downloads, rapid manufacturing processes and interactive production platforms allow customers to choose colours, materials and designs of such items as jeans, shoes and bags (see pages 136–39). Customization creates garments that have a better fit, and the ability to co-craft them with designers gives customers a say about how the clothes look and perform. With consumers personally involved in design and manufacturing processes, goods, services and experiences can more efficiently be tailored to meet their needs.

Feedback fashion

Many people who buy fashion enjoy showing off their creative skills and sharing their thoughts about clothing, and new forums are enabling them to do so. According to British fashion consultancy Franklin Till, which coined the term 'feedback fashion', social media give people the means to share their ideas and fashion preferences and to receive feedback from others. Individuals linked to such networks as Twitter and Facebook, or who use style-orientated apps, can upload pictures of garments they like and obtain crowdsourced feedback on the fashions they are considering buying (see page 186). Brands will use social media to glean feedback on forthcoming collections before they manufacture them, and will enlist celebrities for these types of promotion in order to reach out to their fan base.

Fashion designer Julia Krantz of Sweden collaborated with graphic designer Angela Nilsson and photographer Henrik Bengtsson to develop Tamashii, a design experiment using fashion, packaging, typography and photography, and merging elements of Swedish and Japanese aesthetics.

Generation C clothing

The Generation C phenomenon has emerged as a result of consumer-generated content that individuals are creating online. These people – born after 1990 and seen by trend analysts as being connected, communicators, community-orientated and always 'clicking' – upload terabytes of images, audio, video and text every day, and contribute to real-time content, such as instant-response postings on Twitter. This shift in consumer behaviour is just the excuse fashion brands need to develop web-enabled clothing for mainstream consumers. Consumers' inclination to interface with web content would be facilitated by wearable technology, which would obviate the need for stationary computers and handheld devices in order to remain online. Generation C garments will be the first designs in the emerging genre of techno fashion that will enable wearers to access seamlessly products, services, information and experiences through their clothes.

TECHWEAR

Wearable technology is being engineered to be soft and lightweight, and to feel comfortable against the skin. Embedding portable technology in garments makes it more readily available, and eliminates the need for hard plastic covers or cold metal casings.

Sabine Seymour designs garments capable of what she describes as 'dynamic movement': clothes that project images, scrolling texts and moving motifs. Seymour's research indicates that these capabilities will be standard in the future.

Energy efficiency

Wearable technology will require wearable energy sources. Batteries create health risks that make them too dangerous to wear on the body, leading technologists to develop alternative power sources. Photovoltaic fabrics create energy as they react to light, and are safe to wear. Both of these attributes also apply to crystal-laminate films, which can coat virtually any fabric surface. Crystals, which can easily be embedded into fabric, emit positive and negative ions that can transmit energy electrostatically from power sources to integrated technological parts. In fact, many types of garment and footwear can be engineered to harness the energy expended by the wearer through motion (kinetic energy), and convert it into a power source for wearable technology. Such 'regenerative' fabrics as Energear (page 123) reflect body heat back to the wearer, and this heat could potentially be harnessed to create a power source.

'Gamified' garments

The fun and entertainment of playing games engages individuals and forms lasting links between them. Many consumer brands, service providers and even public-sector amenities currently use gaming as a means of widening their reach, and gaming will become more widespread among fashion brands as a means of building allegiance to the brand. As people play games they explore new ways of experiencing the brand, discover aspects of the collection they may not normally see, build rapport with individuals working for the brand and forge lasting connections with fellow shoppers.

Networked wardrobes

The wardrobe of the future will consist of virtual garments that make it easier to keep track of real clothing. Such technology will help the wearer to combine separates and create new looks (as is possible with My Fashion Plate, page 187), and will be able to recall garments that are stored off-site. Networked wardrobes will also form links with one another, and connect with fashion brands for style updates. Their interconnected reach will make it possible to source garments available for loan or hire, and to ascertain what other people plan to wear to an event. Networked wardrobes will also invite feedback from other people on the network, and automatically keep abreast of the best methods of maintaining and repairing clothes.

Mental and emotional states can be monitored by this wireless electroencephalograph (EEG) headband, designed by Belgian medical technology developer IMEC. The data can then be transmitted wirelessly to a remote system that recommends ways to improve the wearer's mood.

Technological synthesis

Many of the distinctions between garments and technologized devices will blur, if not disappear completely. As the hard casing of computers gives way to the soft folds of fabric and technological convergence occurs in fashion, garments will become the most popular hardware components within the platform created by information technology and communications networks. Wearable computers will have visible signifiers, but at the microscopic level they will have terascale and nanoscale devices. Future fashions will contain supercomputers small enough to fit on the head of a fibre, and nanoscale robots smaller than a human cell. Such wearable systems will possess cerebral capabilities: cognition, logic and decision-making abilities. They will mimic the body's behaviour, and will be able to recognize the wearer's actions and react by creating a chemical change or triggering a set of preprogrammed instructions.

BRAND BRAVADO

The influence of brands over consumers will rise to new heights in the future, as fashion chains expand their range of services in order to play a bigger role in customers' everyday lives. Clothing will be sold as part of incentives that pamper and entertain customers, and provide lifestyle 'solutions'.

Authenticity

Counterfeit goods have become so common in fashion that they have created a secondary market, in which some people deliberately shop for fakes and 'knock-offs' rather than paying for the original. New manufacturing processes and novel scanning technologies, such as those mentioned in the Future Fabrications chapter (pages 130–67), give fashion brands a way to fight back. Future garments and merchandise will be encoded with information about their origins and materials, giving them a DNA-like signature. By the same token, brands will be subject to greater accountability as consumers become able to identify the materials used in manufacture and to trace most stages of the production cycle. Information encoded in RFID-embedded merchandise (see pages 188–91) will enable people to verify the provenance of anything they buy.

Brand spaces

Building on a trend for retailers to conceive their units as spaces for 'being' where customers can relax in reclining chairs, congregate in semi-private spaces and find free downloads, fashion companies will create similar spaces to promote their brand. People will have scope to hang out and relax in fashion-branded spaces, where they will have opportunities to discover new aspects of the brand. Some fashion houses will invite members of the public to co-design these spaces, gauging people's expectations in order to become part of their lifestyle. Such spaces will provide consumers with an alternative to the home and the office, offering meeting rooms, workstations and many of the comforts of home.

On-site solutions

As fashion brands begin to 'pop up' in temporary locations and expand to include concierge-type services, they will identify and address the problems that fashion can attempt to solve. In the future, fashion brands will cater for a wider variety of their customers' needs than they do at present, becoming mobile in order to provide the type of clothing appropriate to the places the shoppers visit. A shoe brand, for example, may park a mobile kiosk selling comfortable footwear outside a nightclub so that people can slip aching feet into cushiony shoes after a long night of dancing, and vending machines stocked with fresh garments and practical accessories will be installed in powder rooms.

Comme des Garçons was one of the first fashion labels to use retail spaces as a means of surprising its customers. The company created luxury interiors in run-down spaces and launched pop-up shops in unexpected locations, and it established Dover Street Market in London as a uniquely branded space that also stocks merchandise from other labels.

MADE TO MUTATE

Visionary manufacturing techniques, new finishing processes and high-tech fabrics can give garments the potential to alter their shape and appearance. Materials engineered to absorb impact, reconfigure their surfaces and change temperature will become widespread.

Julia Krantz's garments shape the fashioned body into otherworldly silhouettes, even giving it an insectoid appearance; pictured here is a piece from her Shell collection, part of her final-year college project. As inspiration begins to emerge from biomimicry, robotics, genetic modification and combat uniforms, future garments are likely to take on some surprising shapes.

Deterioration by design

Manufacturers of all sorts often build planned obsolescence into their products, but few items are designed to make the process of deterioration appealing. In the future, garments created with longevity in mind and designed to have continued appeal as they show signs of wear and tear would be made with robust materials and layered surface coatings engineered to erode with use, revealing new patterns underneath. Certain types of garment, such as jeans, could be customized and ordered new, then 'broken in' by being pre-worn by others. Such products will blur the boundaries between second-hand clothing and new fashion items.

Fifth-season fashions

People currently dress in response to weather patterns and seasonal temperatures, yet many of us foray into climate-controlled interiors for which seasonal clothing is not suited. The American art and fashion historian Richard Martin conceived a year-round wardrobe that would reduce the need to buy different clothing types for different times of year, enabling the wearer to create a 'fifth season' of climate-responsive clothing. Garments containing such innovations as phase-change materials (page 119), shape-shifting fabrics and textiles that condense and thicken (see pages 112 and 113) will surpass the seasons, and people will wear clothing that senses temperature changes and adjusts automatically.

Illusion wear

Garments have traditionally consisted of two-dimensional designs that outline the body's contours, but new design technology will make it possible to mask the wearer's shape. The emerging field of 'illusion wear' manipulates fashion patterns and garment designs in ways that appear to modify the wearer's proportions. Such garments currently use optical illusions to highlight certain areas and detract attention from others, making the wearer appear slimmer, more toned or more shapely. Future designs will feature electronic-screen-like surfaces that reconfigure to create the wearer's desired illusions. The garments will be able to mimic the appearance of a variety of materials (such as water, as in Iris van Herpen's Crystallization collection of Spring/ Summer 2011; see page 219), textures, colours and motifs.

Tailored protection

The demand for protective clothing is on the rise as urban dwellers cycle through the city, walk through areas affected by crime and feel vulnerable when confronted by some of the challenges of crowded city life. Clothing made from soft materials that rigidify on impact (see pages 84–86 and 110–12) can endow everyday clothing with resilience and strength, yet look like conventional clothing. Urban dwellers want the protective value of such clothing, yet will look for it in the form of tailored garments. Future protective garments will look like conventional sportswear or well-cut uniforms; those designed for cycling will resemble stylish urban clothing.

Transformables

Transformable garments bring utility and multifunctionality to fashion, giving the wardrobe roles beyond its wearable potential. Wearable technology will endow clothing with communication capacities and a range of other attributes, but consumers will look to clothing to fulfil other practical functions, too. Transformable fashions (such as the JakPak jacket, page 163) can assume the form of furniture and shelter today, but in the future they will be likely to morph into other types of material goods, and change shape to perform robot-like tasks.

Future garments may be created from liquid solutions that harden to form a dress (as imagined by Nancy Tilbury; see page 27) then revert to their fluid state before forming another garment. This piece from Iris van Herpen's Crystallization collection of Spring/Summer 2011, which appears to be in a state of transition from one design to another, seems to capture this futuristic methodology.

RAPID REJUVENATION

Future clothing will feature coatings and materials that make the wearer feel revitalized and appear refreshed. Smudges, stains and spills on the garment's surface will vanish, while vitamins and stimulants in the lining will be absorbed by the skin.

Multisensory 'skins'

Garments equipped with sensing abilities will be programmed to identify certain stimuli in the environment, enabling them to 'see', 'smell' and 'feel' things that the wearer may not be able to. They will detect changes in temperature and weather and respond accordingly, and scan airborne particles for invisible pollutants. They will also glean information on physiological symptoms from the wearer and nearby individuals, sensing and reacting to emotional states. These sensory garments will form links with one another, as humans do, perhaps even giving parents real-time information about their child's well-being and physical proximity. Programmed with health-care applications, their diagnostic abilities will make them a constituent of wearable wellness (see opposite).

Personal purification

Today, fashion is attempting to lose its reputation for using toxic production methods and for polluting landfill, and is aligning itself with clarity, freshness and integrity. Future fashion will continue to advance the quest for permanently clean clothing and footwear, even to the extent that some will be said to 'purify' the wearer and the environment. Clothing similar to Helen Storey's air-purifying jeans (pages 158 and 160–61), which are made from fibres that filter the air around them, will be able to neutralize pollutants so that they do not come into contact with the wearer's skin. No-wash clothing will be popular at first (see right), but people will come to doubt that these garments can really remain truly clean. As a result, fashion brands will hit back with ranges of clothes so crisp and clean that, thanks to the bacteria-eating antimicrobial preparations they contain, they will actually sanitize the wearer as they come into contact with the skin.

Wash-free fashion

One of the most revolutionary developments in textile design today is the application of coatings that create surfaces so slick that dirt molecules cannot adhere to them. Developed by researchers in the nanotechnology sector, the coatings are bonded to the fabric at fibre level, making them durable enough to withstand wear and tear and exposure to sunshine and rain. Fabrics that can repel dirt and liquids (such as Schoeller's NanoSphere; page 125) will remain clean for as long as the coatings with which they are treated remain active. Not only will such clothing be self-cleaning, but the garments will also be stain-resistant and remain crisp without ironing.

Nancy Tilbury's vision for future fashion includes genetically engineered garments that can be grown on the body. Clothing that issues from the skin will be refreshed as the skin regenerates, and, in the manner of other body parts, will react to sensory stimuli.

Wearable wellness

Remote health monitoring will be the key to better quality of life in old age. Many of the technologies currently under development for specialist medical, military combat, performance and sportswear applications will be made into wearable technology for general use. Fashion will provide a conduit for mobile medical systems that will monitor the wearer, but they will have the look and feel of normal garments. Future wearable materials will medicate the wearer (see iLoad, page 125), and will also contain sensors that will diagnose problems and relay information to health-care practitioners. Fabrics will be equipped with contaminant-aware substances that detect signs of infection, or alert wearers to the presence of infectious agents. The demand for garments suited to health-care applications is already resulting in clothing with hidden openings that make things easier and more comfortable for patients undergoing treatments that require intravenous lines, such as dialysis and chemotherapy. In the future, wearing garments impregnated with dietary supplements, stimulants and anti-ageing products will be as popular as swallowing vitamin tablets is today.

TRANS-HUMAN TOMORROWS

The technological revolution is transforming both fashion as we know it and the fashioned body. Wearable technology will create symbiosis between the body and the machine, giving the wearer potential beyond what is generally conceived of as human. Similar to cyborgs, the man–machine hybrids that technologized clothing will create promise to blur the boundaries between human capability and artificial intelligence. Future body ideals will be based on the heroes of science fiction more than they will reflect true human physiques, and we will demonstrate superhero strength, speed and stealth.

Twenty-first-century fashion is currently becoming aligned with ambitions to maximize the body's potential, enhancing the performance of athletes and enabling bodies to heal more quickly, look slimmer and feel fresher. Before long, garments will revitalize and rejuvenate the body, boost blood circulation, medicate the skin and monitor vital signs. They will link wirelessly to multimedia platforms and forge vast networks among wearers. Clothing will hold the potential to equip the body with completely new skills and augment existing ones, greatly enhancing intellectual and psychological capacities as they boost our physical well-being. Future fashion will reflect what we humans know to be true about ourselves: that we have the potential to be more than we allow ourselves to be.

As fashion becomes inextricably linked with human achievement, it becomes aligned with humanistic values that contribute to society as a whole. Wearable technology will differ from ordinary computing devices by providing ways to assist individuals as they pursue personal happiness and their own self-interests. They will be programmed to embody our highest aspirations and will provide the means to transform our everyday experiences. Fashion will facilitate the creation of group dynamics, connecting individuals with one another and forming social networks.

Future fashion will enable humans to transcend the boundaries of what we currently think we can achieve. As a result, the generation of fashion consumers that emerges may be regarded as transcendent humans, individuals whose technologically enhanced abilities approach the futuristic concept of the hypothetical post-human. Such trans-humans, as they may come to be known (the term was coined in 1949 by French philosopher Pierre Teilhard de Chardin), will cross the threshold to a new kind of existence. They will adapt all technology for wear on the human body. The garments that result will be used in extraordinary ways; yet they will be worn by real people, in everyday situations. Future fashions will evolve into forms unimaginable today, and many of the limitations human beings currently face will become things of the distant past.

OPPOSITE
Wearable technology will cause body ideals to evolve in future, even to the extent that they will reflect a symbiosis between humans and the technologies they use. The new relationships between people, their surroundings, the devices they employ and the way they communicate with one another will go beyond what is generally conceived of today. With its winglike raglan sleeves, this garment from Iris van Herpen's Escapism collection of Autumn/Winter 2011–12 creates a silhouette that seems more celestial than human.

PAGES 224–25
In her Morphogenesis collection of 2010, Pauline van Dongen explored the interaction between people and their surroundings, and the void between the body and the garment, which is emphasized by the use of such contrasting materials as synthetic crin (horsehair) and buntal (extracted from the buri palm tree). Alienating shapes float around the body, creating a sharp, minimalist feel.

ANNE MARIE COMMANDEUR

Dutch trend expert Anne Marie Commandeur is based in Amsterdam, but her work is global in its reach. Charting emerging trends in fashion, textiles and product design as they unfold enables her to forecast what consumers will buy in five years' time. Commandeur has been in the forecasting business since 1987, when she set up her own trend studio. In 2004 she established Stijlinstituut Amsterdam, a forecasting agency that monitors fashion trends, consumer behaviour, technological developments and new directions in product design. Commandeur uses her findings as a basis for creating marketing strategies, communication campaigns and retail formulas, and produces trend concepts for cutting-edge fashions, interior designs, cosmetics and textiles. In the following interview, Commandeur's fast-paced projections suggest that fashion is moving forward less quickly than many other creative areas. As she identifies some of the things that may be slowing fashion's progress, she nonetheless feels that a revolutionary new generation of clothing is on the way.

What needs to happen in order to enable fashion to move forward?

There is a gap between technology and design today that needs to be closed. Although fibre technology is extremely sophisticated, there are hardly any design features factored into the process or end product. Textile technologists often overlook the opportunities to engineer a high-quality product so that it includes a design aesthetic, meaning that few textile companies get the best out of their machinery and resources. Because few designers have a voice in the production of fabric, they simply accept that the product being sold is the best that it can be. This calls for a more creative approach to be integrated in the technical part of the process.

Design thinking should be fully integrated into the process of fibre and fabric technology; it should be used to calibrate the machinery and shape the dyeing and finishing processes. I hope designers become aware of these issues, so that they realize they can have input into the development of the textiles they buy, and that they can help to make fabrics more sustainable, ethical and economical as a result.

Is the divide between technology and design really so pronounced?

Absolutely. Designers are welcome to source materials at fabric exhibitions around the world, but they are not invited to visit the technical textile events, or the machinery and equipment trade fairs. In their current forms, these events are of no interest to designers, but if designers were encouraged to visit them they could have input at a grass-roots level. Once the divide between industrial manufacturing and design creativity has been closed, textile production will emerge as a fully integrated and collaborative process.

Do you mean that the gap between technology and design is hindering fashion's evolution?

You could say that technology is advancing rapidly in all areas of design – apart from fashion. From what we know about ancient cultures, fabric and garments have been woven and stitched for at least 7000 years. Today it is possible to make non-woven materials, use seamless production methods and fabricate garments by 3D printing processes, yet most garments continue to be made by knitting, weaving, stitching and seaming.

So fashion, compared to other industries, is practically standing still. Is this because of consumer needs? Is fashion's evolution the last taboo? Or has technology failed? The answer to all three questions is 'no'. The explanation is that the main components of the fashion industry are all on strictly separate tracks. Textile technology, textile designs, garment manufacturing, finishers, fashion designers and now scientific researchers work without a common platform that would enable them to build bridges between these processes. This blocks the road towards a revolutionary generation of garments.

What will consumers expect in the future?

Consumers will want it all, and want it fast. They will want simple solutions. This is not so much about the shape of the product – I am not talking about basics here – as about the way it presents itself. The garment can be high-tech, intricately made and fabricated in advanced materials, yet it should provide a simple solution. Consumers are less keen to amass more and

Together with her colleagues at Stijlinstituut Amsterdam, Anne Marie Commandeur produces inspirational graphics to illustrate new directions emerging in the fashion and lifestyle sectors. The visual spreads shown here depict new seasonal colours and textures, and showcase inspirations from nature and craft. Both were produced for *Textile View* magazine.

These images are taken from a video Commandeur made about new printing technologies. Modern fibre technology, together with heat-sensitive dyes and photo-reactive coatings, could enable garments to change motifs as they respond to body heat or daylight.

more stuff, yet they want solutions that enable them to live the life they have chosen to live. In turn, the role of the designer will be reassessed completely. Instead of using their creativity constantly to deliver new and more product, designers should think about finding the need, the niche and the gap, about creating products that provide real solutions rather than objects that will be used once and then discarded.

What will the study and forecasting of trends be like in the future?

As it is now, forecasting will be an outcome of many types of analysis, such as consumer analysis, product and design research and market research. Our role is to research our audiences before we decide on ways to communicate trends. Our storylines should be tailored and well timed. There is not a fixed guide or manual for the coming seasons that lists a clear-cut set of trends matching the needs of all manufacturers, segments and regions. Clarity and a sense of realism are needed, as well as an open mind, versatility and creativity. Diversification, flexibility and personalization are key, and they create a need for clear paths in order to move forward.

Which megatrends are most instrumental in shaping fashion's future?

There are many, but here are five I consider to be important right now.

Transparency in fashion chain management is a very important feature and

a vast challenge. This will ask for ultimate attention from the business, since consumers look for trusted suppliers and don't want to be bothered with all the details. Yet there should be a clear and open track record for consumers to look into as soon as they spot trouble.

Ease will be important. This covers ease of access to all fashion items needed, as well as easy maintenance of the garments.

Escapism provides consumers with space to dream. They are in need of wonderlands, of routes on which to switch off from their everyday stresses. Designers will have to continue to dazzle and surprise, to entertain. The big risk in these times of uncertainty is to focus too closely on consumer-expressed needs. Simply satisfying needs would entail no risk; yet at the same time it would achieve no progress, bring about no change and introduce no future, because people need a sense of anticipation.

Flexibility is required from designers to address the need for fashion products that allow consumers to create, interact, influence. Fashion designers can better address consumer needs by providing toolkits, ingredients and direct access to manufacturing processes or printing equipment, and creating open-source design or production platforms. On the other hand, all this should be fast, simple to use and user-friendly.

Added value will be continually in demand. Consumers will want products that provide added value by boosting vitality, looks or performance.

DIRECTORY

A

Advansa
advansa.com

Kelsey Ashe
ashestore.com.au

B

Bak2u
bak2u.com

Neil Barrett
neilbarrett.com

Janine Benyus/Biomimicry 3.8
janinebenyus.com
biomimicry.net

Biocouture
biocouture.co.uk

Biodevices SA
biodevices.pt

Bodymetrics
bodymetrics.com

C

CASPIAN
nocards.org

Celanese Corporation
celanese.com

CETEMMSA
cetemmsa.com

Hussein Chalayan
husseinchalayan.com

Bernard Chandran
bernardchandran.com

Andreia Chaves
andreiachaves.com

Shao-Yen Chen
shao-yen.com

Jimmy Choo
jimmychoo.com

Clemens en August
clemens-en-august.com

Closet Infinite
closetinfinite.wordpress.com

Cocona
coconainc.com

Colorep
colorep.com

Anne Marie Commandeur/
Stijlinstituut Amsterdam
stijlinstituut.nl

Comme des Garçons
comme-des-garcons.com

Commonwealth Scientific and
Industrial Research
Organisation
csiro.au

Country Road
countryroad.com.au

CuteCircuit
cutecircuit.com

D

Dainese
dainese.com

DARPA (Defense Advanced
Research Projects Agency)
darpa.mil

Descente
descente.com

Sheree Dornan
shereedornan.com

Dow Corning
dowcorning.com

Dream Heels
dreamheels.com

D3O
d3o.com

DuPont
renewable.dupont.com

DuPont Tate & Lyle
duponttateandlyle.com

E

Eeonyx Corporation
eeonyx.com

Elemental Threads
elementalthreads.com

Eley Kishimoto
eleykishimoto.com

EmmaActive
emmaactive.com

Diana Eng
dianaeng.com

F

Fabrican/Manel Torres
fabricanltd.com

Filippa K
filippa-k.com

Fits.Me
fits.me

FranklinTill
franklintill.com

Freedom Of Creation
freedomofcreation.com

G

Go Try It On
gotryiton.com

Grado Zero Espace
gzespace.com

H

Zaha Hadid Architects
zaha-hadid.com

Amila Hrustic
amila.ba

Hyod
hyod-products.com

Hypertag
hypertag.com

I

IMEC
imec.be

Indi Custom
indicustom.com

It's My Scar
itsmyscar.com

J

JakPak
jakpak.com

Maria Janssen/WGSN
wgsn.com/?=experts/58

Eunjeong Jeon
crash.curtin.edu.au/research/
groups/body/eunjeongjeon.cfm

K

Tobie Kerridge and Nikki Stott
biojewellery.com

Kisim
kisim.com

Konarka
konarka.com

L

Looklet
looklet.com

M

William McDonough
mcdonough.com

Lucy McRae and Bart Hess
lucyandbart.blogspot.com

Microtrace
microtracesolutions.com

Issey Miyake
isseymiyake.com

N

Natick Soldier Research,
Development and Engineering
Center (NSRDEC)
nsrdec.natick.army.mil

NeuroFocus
neurofocus.com

Nike
nike.com

NuMetrex
numetrex.com

O

Oakley
oakley.com

Ohmatex
ohmatex.dk

Marie O'Mahony
uts.edu.au (staff directory)

O'Neill
oneill.com

Onitsuka Tiger
onitsukatiger.com

Maggie Orth
maggieorth.com

Outlast
outlast.com

P

Despina Papadopoulos
5050ltd.com

Philips Design
design.philips.com

P2i
p2i.com

Gareth Pugh
garethpugh.net

Pull-in
pull-in.com

R

The Red Rail
theredrail.com

Reebok
reebok.com

Rip Curl
ripcurl.com

Kevin Roberts
lovemarks.com

S

Sans
sans.name

Schoeller
schoeller-textiles.com

Serfontaine
serfontaine.com

Sabine Seymour/Moondial
moondial.com

Shiseido
shiseido.com

ShockDoctor
shockdoctor.com

Shoes of Prey
shoesofprey.com

Skin Graph
skingraph.wordpress.com

smartfiber
smartfiber.de

Speedo
speedo.com

Charles Spence
psyweb.psy.ox.ac.uk/xmodal

Spyder Active Sports
spyder.com

Storage By Mail
storagebymail.com

Helen Storey
helenstoreyfoundation.org

T

Susumu Tachi
tachilab.org

Teijin Fibers
teijinfiber.com

Tikaro/p8tches
p8t.ch

Nancy Tilbury
studiotilbury.com
studio-xo.com

Touchatag
touchatag.com

Kosuke Tsumura
finalhome.com

U

Ultra
weareultra.com

V

Vacant
govacant.com

Pauline van Dongen
paulinevandongen.com

Iris van Herpen
irisvanherpen.com

W

Moritz Waldemeyer
waldemeyer.com

Adam Whiton and Yolita Nugent
no-contact.com

X

X-Technology
x-technology.com

Z

Zelfo Technology
zelfo-technology.com

Xiang Zhang
xlab.me.berkeley.edu

BIBLIOGRAPHY

Marc Augé, *Non-Places: Introduction to an Anthropology of Supermodernity*, London (Verso) 1995

Janine Benyus, *Biomimicry: Innovation Inspired by Nature*, New York (Harper Perennial) 2002

Simon Bowen, *A Critical Artefact Methodology: Using Provocative Conceptual Designs to Foster Human-centred Innovation*, PhD dissertation, Sheffield Hallam University, 2009

Svetlana Boym, *The Future of Nostalgia*, New York (Basic Books) 2002

Sarah Braddock Clarke and Marie O'Mahony, *Techno Textiles: Revolutionary Fabrics for Fashion and Design*, London (Thames & Hudson) 1999

—, *Techno Textiles 2: Revolutionary Fabrics for Fashion and Design*, London (Thames & Hudson) 2005

D. Branson and M. Sweeney, 'Conceptualization and Measurement of Clothing Comfort: Toward a Metatheory', in *Critical Linkages in Textiles and Clothing Subject Matter: Theory, Method and Practice*, ed. S.B. Kaiser and M.L. Damhorst, International Textile and Apparel Association (ITAA), 1991, pp. 94–105

Patrizia Calefato, *The Clothed Body*, Oxford (Berg) 2004

Chloë Colchester, *Textiles Today: A Global Survey of Trends and Traditions*, London (Thames & Hudson) 2007

Matthew B. Crawford, *Shop Class as Soulcraft: An Inquiry into the Value of Work*, New York (Penguin) 2010

Rasshied Din, *New Retail*, London (Conran Octopus) 2000

Caroline Evans, Suzy Menkes, Ted Polhemus and Bradley Quinn, *Hussein Chalayan*, Rotterdam (Groninger Museum/NAI) 2005

James Jerome Gibson, *The Ecological Approach to Visual Perception*, London (Lawrence Erlbaum) 1979

Ingrid Giertz-Mårtenson, *Att se in i framtiden. En studie av trendanalys inom modebranschen* (Looking into the Future: An Analysis of Fashion Forecasting), Stockholm (Department of Ethnology, Stockholm University) 2006

Jane Harris, *Surface Tension – The Aesthetic Fabrication of Digital Textiles: The Design and Construction of 3D Computer Graphic Animation*, PhD dissertation, Royal College of Art, London, 2000

Caroline Hummels, *Gestural Design Tools: Prototypes, Experiments and Scenarios*, PhD dissertation, Delft University of Technology, 2000

Eunjeong Jeon, 'Aesthetic Experience and Comfort: The Relationship Between Semantic Form and Body Movement of the Design of Wool Clothing', International Association of Societies of Design Research conference: *Rigor and Relevance in Design*, Seoul, 18–22 October 2009, crash.curtin.edu.au/research/groups/body/EJ_Jeon_Doctoral%20Colloquium_IASDR09.pdf (accessed 31 October 2011)

—, 'Object Playing with Movement: A Source of Comfort and Enjoyment', International Association of Societies of Design Research conference: *Rigor and Relevance in Design*, Seoul, 18–22 October 2009, crash.curtin.edu.au/research/groups/body/EJ_Jeon_IASDR09.2009.pdf (accessed 2 November 2011)

S. Klooster and K. Overbeeke, 'Designing Products as an Integral Part of Choreography of Interaction: The Product's Form as an Integral Part of Movement', *Design and Semantics of Form and Movement* (DeSForM) conference, Eindhoven, 11 November 2005, alexandria.tue.nl/repository/books/634465.pdf (accessed 2 November 2011)

Harold Koda, *Extreme Beauty: The Body Transformed*, New York (The Metropolitan Museum of Art) 2001

Suzanne Lee, *Fashioning the Future: Tomorrow's Wardrobe*, London (Thames & Hudson) 2007

William McDonough and Michael Braungart, *Cradle to Cradle: Remaking the Way We Make Things*, Emmaus, Pa. (Rodale Books) 2003

A.K. Pradeep, *The Buying Brain: Secrets for Selling to the Unconscious Mind*, Hoboken, NJ (John Wiley and Sons) 2010

Bradley Quinn, *Design Futures*, London (Merrell) 2011

—, *The Fashion of Architecture*, Oxford (Berg) 2003

—, *Techno Fashion*, Oxford (Berg) 2002

—, *Textile Futures*, Oxford (Berg) 2010

—, ed., *Ultra Materials*, London (Thames & Hudson) 2007

Brent Dean Robbins, 'Emotion, Movement & Psychological Space: A Sketching Out of the Emotions in Terms of Temporality, Spatiality, Embodiment, Being-with, and Language', mythosandlogos.com, 2009, mythosandlogos.com/emotion.html (accessed 22 September 2011)

Gabriel Robles-De-La-Torre, 'The Importance of the Sense of Touch in Virtual and Real Environments', *IEEE Multimedia* 13, 2006, pp. 24–30

Sabine Seymour, *Functional Aesthetics: Visions in Fashionable Technology*, Vienna (Springer) 2010

Lieva van Langenhove, ed., *Smart Textiles for Medicine and Healthcare: Materials, Systems and Applications*, Cambridge (Woodhead Publishing and CRC Press) 2007

Henrik Vejlgaard, *Anatomy of a Trend*, New York (McGraw-Hill) 2007

Jayne Wallace, *Emotionally Charged: A Practice-centred Enquiry of Digital Jewellery and Personal Emotional Significance*, PhD dissertation, Sheffield Hallam University, 2007

ACKNOWLEDGEMENTS

This book would not have been possible without the support of the designers and researchers featured in it. I thank each one of them for giving generously of their time to provide images of and information about their work. Noriko Nishiya, Mette Mitchell and Ingrid Giertz-Mårtenson are among the friends who helped me to source information and track down designers, and my consultancy colleagues within Odyssey Network made me aware of new consumer demands and innovations in manufacturing and retail. I should also like to thank the book's editors and art directors for their commitment to the project, and for being so delightful to work with.

Fashion Futures is dedicated to Fran Synge Clark, a friend of long standing who has always inspired me with her edgy approaches to fashion. An athlete, Fran keeps everyone updated on developments in sportswear. As a fashionista and interiors aficionado, she once famously decorated her New York East Village apartment with the season's trend colours, coordinating her wardrobe and interior in shades of bright yellow, lime-green and cherry-pink.

PICTURE CREDITS

l = left; r = right; t = top; b = bottom;
c = centre

Haider Ackermann/Dan and Corina Lecca: 33, 203; AFP/Getty Images: 80; Ezzidin Alwan/Nancy Tilbury: 34–35; Kelsey Ashe: 183 (top row); Thierry Berrod, Mona Lisa Production/Science Photo Library: 111t; Randy Brooke/AirDye/Costello Tagliapietra: 102 (both); Catwalking.com: 79, 85; Bernard Chandran/Christopher Dadey: 8, 159; Andreia Chaves/Andrew Bradley: 31; Shao-Yen Chen/Nicole Maria Winkler: 127, 142–43; Jimmy Choo: 157; Cocona Inc: 104; Ian Cole/Fabrican Ltd/Dr Manel Torres: 146, 147; Anne Marie Commandeur: 227, 228; Atton Conrad: 22, 23; CSIRO: 107r; Perry Curties/Nancy Tilbury: 221; D3O/All-Star: 71t, 71b, 86t; D3O/Furygan: 73; D3O/Icon: 86b, 112; Sheree Dornan: 183 (bottom row); courtesy Dover Street Market: 176–77, 214–15; DuPont: 75, 76tl, 76tr, 76b, 105c; Gavin Duthie: 160–61; Douglas Eng/Diana Eng: 98, 107c, 109, 120r; eThreads: 138t, 138c; Fits.me: 185; FOC: 144–45 (all); Go Try It On: 186 (all); Pascal Goetgheluck/Science Photo Library: 111b; James Graham/Diana Eng: 95; Zaha Hadid Architects/Photography Virgile Simon Bertrand: 171, 195 (all), 196–97; Amila Hrustic (design)/Irfan Redzovic (photography): jacket, front endpaper, 39, 48, 49; Hufton + Crow/View: 172; Hufton + Crow/View/Corbis: 173; Hyod: 67, 87b; Hypertag: 189 (both); IMEC: 120l, 212; Indi/Bonnie Coombs: 136t, 136c; Jonas Ingerstedt (photography)/Hövding Sverige

AB (design): 68–69; JakPak: 162 (all); Maria Janssen/WGSN: 89; Eunjeong Jeon/Kyunghoon Kim: 43; Jens Kalaene/dpa/Corbis: 175b; Julia Krantz/Henrik Bengtsson: 209; Julia Krantz/Garri Frischer: 24, 25; Julia Krantz/Katrin Kirojood: 217; Kuchofuku: 26l; Ellie Laycock/Nancy Tilbury: 63, 64; Suzanne Lee: 141; Richard Levine/Alamy: 175t; Jeffrey Lipton (Fab@Home Project): 148; Rick Louis/Diana Eng: 96, 97, 100–101 (all), 121; Aoife Ludlow: 136b; Luminex S.p.A.: 108c; Microtrace/Ron Goldman: 115r; Christopher More/Catwalking.com: 201; Kenn Munk: 192, 193 (both); My Fashion Plate: 187 (all); NuMetrex: 82r, 82b; Ohmatex: 108r; Marie O'Mahony: 129 (both); O'Neill: 82tl; O'Neill/Mike Coots: 117 (both); Onitsuka Tiger: 178; Maggie Orth/International Fashion Machines: 21; Rick Owens/Marco Madeira: 16–17 (all), 40, 41, 205; Rick Owens/Owenscorp: 83; P2i 2011: 116; Despina Papadopoulos/Studio 5050: 20 (both); Philips Design: 37, 207; Pierre Proske/Voiceprints: 133 (all); pull-in.com/blackleaf.com: 91tl, 91br; ripcurl.com: 91tr, 91bl; Rohner/SmartFiber AG: 105l; sans.name/Lika Volkova and Alessandro DeVito (design): 138bl, 138br; Schoeller Textil AG: 114, 115c, 119l, 123l, 123r, 125l, 125r; Sabine Seymour/Moondial: 99, 165 (all), 211; Irina Shaposhnikova: 30; Irina Shaposhnikova/Etienne Tordoir/Catwalkpictures: 46 (all), 202; shoesofprey.com: 137 (all); Skin Graph: 139, 167; Tim Smit: 59; Steven Smith, U.S. Army Natick Soldier Research,

Development and Engineering Center: 77 (all); Spider Silk: 113; Spyder Active Sports, Inc: 70, 87t; Studio XO/Tom Banks: 52, 53, 54t, 55; Studio XO/Ethan Miller/Getty Images for ABC: 54b; [TC]²: 150–51 (all); Nancy Tilbury: 26r, 27, 140; © TOTeM: 191 (all); Scott Trindle/Gareth Pugh: 2–3, 15 (both); Pauline van Dongen: 134, 135; Pauline van Dongen/Photography Mike Nicolaassen/Hair Tommy Hagen at House of Orange/Make-up Vera Dierckx at House of Orange/Styling April Jumelet/Model Macha at Fresh Model Management: 7; Pauline van Dongen/Photography Mike Nicolaassen/ Hair and make-up Dennis Michael at Angelique Hoorn Agency/ Model Kelly at Ragazza Model Management: 224, 225; Iris van Herpen/Michel Zoeter: 13, 18, 45, 51 (all), 149, 153, 219, 223; Sander Veeneman/No Colors/The Soon Institute: 155, 156; Susanna Vuong/planeshop™: 174, 180, 181; We Are Ultra: 103; Adam Whiton/Yolita Nugent: 28–29 (all), 72 (both), 119r, 124; Witters/Press Association Images: 60–61; Zelfo: 105r.

The publisher has made every effort to trace and contact copyright holders of the material reproduced in this book. It will be happy to correct in subsequent editions any errors or omissions that are brought to its attention.

INDEX

First published 2012 by

Merrell Publishers Limited
81 Southwark Street
London SE1 0HX

merrellpublishers.com

British Library Cataloguing-in-Publication Data:
Quinn, Bradley.
Fashion futures.
1. Fashion design–History–21st century.
I. Title
746.9'2'09051-dc23

ISBN 978-1-8589-4563-7

Produced by Merrell Publishers Limited
Designed by Alexandre Coco
Project-managed by Marion Moisy
Indexed by Vicki Robinson

Typeset in Titillium (campivisivi.net/titillium)
and ITC Officina Sans (itcfonts.com)

Printed and bound in China

BRADLEY QUINN is a London-based writer and
journalist. His work appears regularly in such
magazines and newspapers as *Wallpaper**, *Elle
Decoration* and the *Evening Standard*, while his
many books include *Techno Fashion* (2002), *The
Fashion of Architecture* (2003), *Mid-century Modern*
(2004), *Ultra Materials* (2007), *Textile Designers
at the Cutting Edge* (2009), *Textile Futures* (2010)
and *Design Futures* (Merrell, 2011). He is also a
frequent contributor to trend-forecasting guides,
and produces inspirational concepts for clients
in the creative industries.

FRONT COVER AND FRONT ENDPAPER: From Amila
Hrustic's Plato collection (see pages 39, 48 and 49).
PAGES 2–3: From Gareth Pugh's Spring/Summer
2011 collection (see page 15).

ISBN 978-1-8589-4563-7